The

Year

of the

Poet VI

September 2019

The Poetry Posse

inner child press, ltd.

The Poetry Posse 2019

Gail Weston Shazor

Shareef Abdur Rasheed

Teresa E. Gallion

hülya n. yılmaz

Kimberly Burnham

Tzemin Ition Tsai

Elizabeth Esguerra Castillo

Jackie Davis Allen

Joe Paire

Caroline 'Ceri' Nazareno

Ashok K. Bhargava

Alicja Maria Kuberska

Swapna Behera

Albert 'Infinite' Carrasco

Eliza Segiet

William S. Peters, Sr.

General Information

The Year of the Poet VI
September 2019 Edition

The Poetry Posse

1st Edition : 2019

Publisher Information

1st Edition : Inner Child Press
intouch@innerchildpress.com
www.innerchildpress.com

ISBN-13 : 978-1-970020-88-5 (inner child press, ltd.)

$ 12.99

WHAT WOULD LIFE BE WITHOUT A LITTLE POETRY?

$\mathcal{D}$edication

This Book is dedicated to

Poetry . . .

The Poetry Posse

past, present & future

our Patrons and Readers

the Spirit of our Everlasting Muse

&

the Power of the Pen

to effectuate change!

In the darkness of my life
I heard the music
I danced . . .
and the Light appeared
and I dance

Janet P. Caldwell

Table of Contents

The Poetry Posse

Table of Contents . . . *continued*

September's Featured Poets 113

Foreword

"We are here to awaken from the illusion of our separateness." ~ Thich Nhat Hanh

All contributors in this book craft their poems on one world culture of collective focus every month. While this tradition guides us throughout our shared work, our objective is not about discovering differences. Because we are aware that there is only one entity to which we belong: Humanity. Regardless of the different languages we have acquired and use in our lifetime, and regardless of the geography-specific upbringing to which we each have been exposed, we are one.

The people of The Caucasus who have been marked with their grandiose eras and wars on history's timeline are no exception. For, no matter on what aspect of their past and present lives each of us have written in this month's poetry collection, they deliver one promise to us, through us: The livelihood of our family, called Humanity.

hülya n. yılmaz, Ph.D.

World Healing, World Peace Foundation
human beings for humanity

worldhealingworldpeacefoundation.org

World Healing, World Peace 2020
International Poetry Symposium

Dear Friends & Family . . . Poets, Poetry Lovers & Humanitarians

We are so excited at ICPI, Inner Child Press International, as we have begun to mobilize for the upcoming epic event of the 'World Healing, World Peace 2020 Poetry Symposium'. Our plans are set for April of 2020. This event will be held in Atlantic City, New Jersey.

We are now collecting names, emails and telephone numbers for all potential resources that can make this event a highly successful, and one of significance that will have a resounding effect on our world and humanity at large. We are also looking for volunteers who can assist us in many areas of facilitation in the planning, staging and execution phases. Going forward, we will be speaking with the business, government, foundation and the private sectors for funding, sponsorship and suitable venues. So, if you know anything, or know someone, we welcome your input and insights.

We will begin shortly to put together our international guest list.

Communicate with us via our email at :

worldhealingworldpeace@gmail.com

or

whwpfoundation@gmail.com

Visit the Web Site(s) :

worldhealingworldpeacepoetry.com

worldhealingworldpeacefoundation.org

World Healing, World Peace 2020 Anthology is now open for submissions.

Submit to :

worldhealingworldpeace@gmail.com

Please share this information

Thank You

Inner Child Press International
'building bridges of cultural understanding'

www.innerchildpress.com

Preface

Dear Family and Friends,

Yes I am excited? This year we have aligned our vision with that of UNESCO as it honors and acknowledges a variety of Global Indigenous cultures. We are now in our sixth year of publication. As are on our way to hitting another milestone. Needless to say, I am elated. Our initial vision was to just perform at this level for the year of 2014. Since that time we have had the blessed opportunity to include many other wonderful word artists and storytellers in the Poetry Posse from lands, cultures and persuasions all over the world. We have featured hundreds of additional poets, thereby introducing their poetic offerings to our vast global readership.

In keeping with our effort and vision to expand the awareness of poets from all walks by making this offerings accessible, we at Inner Child Press International will continue to make every volume a FREE Download. The books are also available for purchase at the affordable cost of $7.00 per volume.

In the previous years, our monthly themes were Flowers, Birds, Gemstones, Trees and Past Cultures. This year we have elected to continue the

Cultural theme. In each month's volume you will have the opportunity to not only read at least one poem themed by our Poetry Posse members about such culture, but we have included a few words about the culture in our prologue. The reasoning behind this is that now our poetry has the opportunity to be educational for not only the reader, but we poets as well. We hope you find the poetic offerings insightful as we use our poetic form to relay to you what we too have learned through our research in making our offering available to you, our readership.

In closing, we would like to thank you for being an integral part of our amazing journey.

Enjoy our amazing featured poets . . . they are amazing!

Building Cultural Bridges of Understanding . . .

Bless Up . . . From the home in our hearts to yours

Bill

The Poetry Posse
Inner Child Press Ineternational

PS

Do Not forget about the World Healing, World Peace Poetry effort.

Available here

www.worldhealingworldpeacepoetry.com

For Free Downloads of Previous Issues of The Year of the Poet

www.innerchildpress.com/the-year-of-the-poet

poetry is . . . .

The Caucuses

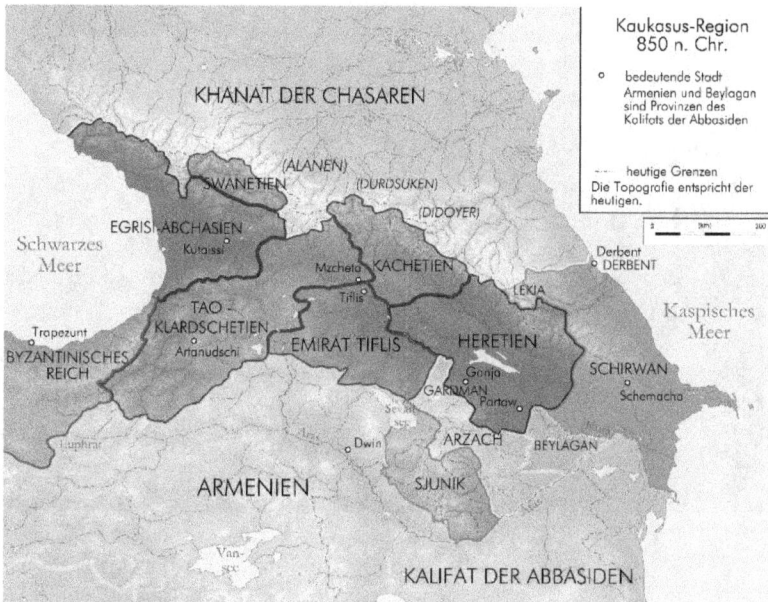

The Caucuses is a region noted by its mountainous geography that lies where Europe and Asia converge. It is also the home of the Caucasian race. From this area came many similar yet distinctive cultural attributes whose peoples migrated into Russia, Europe and Asia as well. This region principally lies between the Caspian and the Black Seas. Armenia, Azerbaijan, Georgia and Russia. The Caucasus Mountains include the Greater and the Lesser Caucasus mountain range. These mountains are seen as a natural barrier that separates Western Asia from Eastern Europe.

For more information . . .
https://en.wikipedia.org/wiki/Caucasus

Poets . . .
sowing seeds in the
Conscious Garden of Life,
that those who have yet to come
may enjoy the Flowers.

Poets, Writers . . . know that we are the enchanting magicians that nourishes the seeds of dreams and thoughts . . . it is our words that entice the hearts and minds of others to believe there is something grand about the possibilities that life has to offer and our words tease it forth into action . . . for you are the Poet, the Writer to whom the Gift of Words has been entrusted . . .

~ wsp

Coming
April 2020

The
World Healing, World Peace
International Poetry Symposium

Stay Tuned

for more information
intouch@innerchildpress.com
'building bridges of cultural understanding'
www.innerchildpress.com

Poetry succeeds where instruction fails.

~ wsp

I Fly

because

... said the Dreamer to the world.

I Can

www.iamjustbill.com

Gail Weston Shazor

This is a creative promise ~ my pen will speak to and for the world. Enamored with letters and respectful of their power, I have been writing for most of my life. A mother, daughter, sister and grandmother I give what I have been given, greatfilledly.

Author of . . .

"An Overstanding of an Imperfect Love"
&
Notes from the Blue Roof

Lies My Grandfathers Told Me

available at Inner Child Press.

www.facebook.com/gailwestonshazor
www.innerchildpress.com/gail-weston-shazor
navypoet1@gmail.com

Caucasus

Ice shining, white snow
My peaks reach toward the heavens
To cover your soul

Hear the drums below
Slowing in the bitter cold
We ever hide you

I am eternal
Without any allegiance
I belong to all

Compline

Water caresses psalmody
Wearing the rough edges away
Smoothing weariness into the
Curves of the porcelain basin
A gurgling cacophony of clean
Blends with twilight cricketsong
Pooling into the deep recesses
At the hollow of my spine

The quality of my pleasure
Outweigh my need to rush
The sensual distillery of lavender
And the smell of your memory
At the bend of my knee
My heart stills to prayers
I am not daunted by unfinished chores
Nor am I troubled any longer
By the rush of daylight minutes

Quietness fits across my shoulders
Like a favorite afghan
Against the summer breeze
An anthem rich in coolness
And solemn in need
My absolution is committed
Into your breast
For I remain eager to see your hue
In iridescent hummingbird wings
And the azure of open seas

Miles stretch into dismissal
A solemnity of confession
Ancient is the desire for comfort
And the completion of togetherness
I would have the feast and the rest
As I enter into this night's slumber
My soul longs to bridge the distance
And finally unite our lives
As I have committed my heart to you

Black Ass Way

I am feeling some kinda
Black ass way
Some kinda
You can't check me today
Like I am planning on sitting
Right the hell here
In this black ass high yella skin
Watching you watching me
Analyzing all that shit
That you don't think I see

I am feeling some kinda
Black ass way
Like a just right potato salad
Made in my pork scented kitchen
And ribs soaked
In Miller high life
For hours overnight
Ready for that black ass grill
In the neighborhood park

I am feeling some kinda
Black ass way
Some kinda fist pumping
Afro wearing, cocoa butter smooth
Dressed in fine clothes
Straight from the runway
By some black ass designer
Working in a white house

I am feeling some kinda
Black ass way

In this year of change
Knowing that I can't be
Marginally fixated by hate
And I am still here
Despite the omissions
And the change from life to death

I am feeling some kinda
Black ass way
And if I disappear
Know that I was everything
And history will bear my story
They let me get learned
So know new tricks are needed
To un-memorize my black ass

Alicja
Maria
Kuberska

.

Alicja Maria Kuberska

Alicja Maria Kuberska – awarded Polish poetess, novelist, journalist, editor. She was born in 1960, in Świebodzin, Poland. She now lives in Inowrocław, Poland.

In 2011 she published her first volume of poems entitled: "The Glass Reality". Her second volume "Analysis of Feelings", was published in 2012. The third collection "Moments" was published in English in 2014, both in Poland and in the USA. In 2014, she also published the novel - "Virtual roses" and volume of poems "On the border of dream". Next year her volume entitled "Girl in the Mirror" was published in the UK and "Love me" , " (Not)my poem" in the USA. In 2015 she also edited anthology entitled "The Other Side of the Screen".

In 2016 she edited two volumes: "Taste of Love" (USA), "Thief of Dreams" (Poland) and international anthology entitled " Love is like Air" (USA). In 2017 she published volume entitled "View from the window" (Poland). She also edits series of anthologies entitled "Metaphor of Contemporary" (Poland)

Her poems have been published in numerous anthologies and magazines in Poland, the USA, the UK, Albania, Belgium, Chile, Spain, Israel, Canada, India, Italy, Uzbekistan, Czech Republic, South Korea and Australia. She was a featured poet of New Mirage Journal (USA) in the summer of 2011.

Alicja Kuberska is a member of the Polish Writers Associations in Warsaw, Poland and IWA Bogdani, Albania. She is also a member of directors' board of Soflay Literature Foundation.

Ararat - biblical story

God smiled again
and his breath like a mighty gale
closed the water reservoirs of the Great Abyss.

The last drops of rain fell from heaven.
Powerful lightning and thunder stopped to crumble the sky.
The waters began to lower slowly and hope appeared.

Angels swept away the stormy clouds and powerful fire.
The furious waves desisted to yank the ark
and the sun afresh shone brightly over the horizon.

The black wings of the raven had no rest.
The white dove brought a gift - a leaf from an olive tree.
God hung a rainbow over the mountain as a sign of the
covenant.

A boat, similar to a nut filled with the nucleus of life,
settled on the slopes of the holy mountain called Ararat
Noah's descendants began their journey on the Earth again.

The Sun

When night ends, the show begins on the scene of sky.

The wind opens curtains made of clouds
- heavy and crimped like Baroque draperies.

 Birds begin to treble and proclaim the arrival of light.

Darkness disappears and night flies away on its black
wings.

The gray of morning slowly gains the pearly shades
and pink cloudlets lead the way on blue sky
for an oncoming solar chariot.

Nirvana

Emptiness and relief.
I do feel almost nothing.

A swarm of intrusive thoughts flew away.
They were like small insects,
squeezing into everywhere.
I have no hope, anxieties or joy.

The dead stars shine above me
and the moon phase is repeated every month.
I observe the metamorphosis of space.

I am a jot of lively matter
and I change with the cycles of nature,
I knock under the principles of time.

My life is like a thin thread.
When it breaks I will leave for unknown destination.
I will cross without fear the threshold of mortality.

Jackie
Davis
Allen

Jackie Davis Allen

Jackie Davis Allen, otherwise known as Jacqueline D. Allen or Jackie Allen, grew up in the Cumberland Mountains of Appalachia. As the next eldest daughter of a coal miner father and a stay at home mother, she was the first in her family to attend and graduate from college. Her siblings, in their own right, are accomplished, though she is the only one, to date, that has discovered the gift of writing.

Graduating from Radford University, with a Bachelors of Science degree in Early Education, she taught in both public and private schools. For over a decade she taught private art classes to children both in her home and at a local Art and Framing Shop where she also sold her original soft sculptured Victorian dolls and original christening gowns.

She resides in northern Virginia with her husband, taking much needed get-aways to their mountain home near the Blue Ridge Mountains, a place that evokes memories of days spent growing up in the Appalachian Mountains.

A lover of hats, she has worn many. Following marriage to her college sweetheart, and as wife, mother, grandmother, teacher, tutor, artist, writer, poet and crafter, she is a lover of art and antiques, surrounding herself, always, with books, seeking to learn more.

In 2015 she authored *Looking for Rainbows, Poetry, Prose and Art*, and in 2017, *Dark Side of the Moon*. Both books of mostly narrative poetry were published by Inner Child Press and were edited by hulya n. yilmaz.

http://www.innerchildpress.com/jackie-davis-allen.php
jackiedavisallen.com

Neighbors, In Name Only

Separated geophysically
From Armenia, and from the Caucasus,
She resides less than
A suburban block away,
From a historical neighbor.
A Turk.

Infected with the wound
Of her ancestors' tragic-demise,
She picks at the scab
Of her inheritance. A way
Of resurrecting, remembering
Their names.

From repository of grief,
Seeking not, nor ever inhaling
Fresh air of forgiveness, peace,
She sows self-same seeds of contempt.
Unwilling, unable to reconcile
Generational pain.

And, of the other, the Turk.
Is she even aware of the other?
Is it not more likely, that
The blamed one, distances herself
From their separate, but
Shared history?

Between Friends, Neighbors

There is a structure, a fence
Down below my garden
It is in need of repair

With intent I have attempted
To do it all by myself
Sadly, I have met with no success

A new plan I have come up with
Indeed, I think it might work
If I am met halfway in the design

And with my neighbor's consent
We agree to build a bridge over
Our differences, and even add a gate

What merit is there in resurrecting
Old grievances, some having roots
More than several generations old

Might not the breach between us
Remain in the past, if we use the tools
Of mutual respect and forgiveness

The Key

When you left,
I knew not what to do.
I knocked on the door
Of comprehension. Demanding

Incessantly, demanding answers
To questions above my head.
Above my ability
To understand. And, yet

I heard the news, yesterday.
You are back in the city.
Of necessity you must have passed
By our apartment.

Remember?
You still have the key.
You need not worry.
I have not changed the lock.

Tzemin Ition Tsai

Dr. Tzemin Ition Tsai (蔡澤民博士) was born in Republic of China, in 1957. He holds a Ph.D. in Chemical Engineering and two Masters of Science in Applied Mathematics and Chemical Engineering. He is a professor at Asia University (Taiwan), editor of "Reading, Writing and Teaching" academic text. He also writes the long-term columns for Chinese Language Monthly in Taiwan.

He is a scholar with a wide range of expertise, while maintaining a common and positive interest in science, engineering and literature member.

He has won many national literary awards. His literary works have been anthologized and published in books, journals, and newspapers in more than 40 countries and have been translated into more than a dozen languages.

Dreaming In The Isolated Island Of Christ

When I faced one after another sparkish faces
Gazing at you
Eyes full of curiosity
Just like a clear spring
The dust in my heart
has fallen
Everything from outside
In the world of children
All were magical and wonderful
Although Armenia has a tragic history
Unheeded on the international arena
But such a country
People's faces are filled with laughter and enthusiasm
People's eyes are full of beautiful aspirations
The positive, optimistic, and cheerful nature of this ethnic
group
Even from a child can be seen

Just like her neighbors
Beautiful sceneries, romantic beauties
Winding mountains, lush forest-peaks
Magnificent valleys, Peerless deep gullies
Ancient and elegant churched
All kinds of styles but beautiful
Armenia
She was not known in the international community.
The first Christian country in the world
Foreigners continue to invade and oppress
My relatives and friends heard that I went to Armenia.
Unbelievable eyes wide
But they didn't know when I heard at the Ganard monastery
Historical pain

Coming from their mouths
My expression was just as amazed as them

Strolling on the streets of Yerevan in the summer day
In addition to the gentle breeze
Huge and exaggerated bronze cast pillar statue
Stone step goes up
Beautiful squares, museums, gardens, statues of the 19th
century
The lady taking photos with me at the Yerevan Opera
House
Obviously
Conquered by the kind and subtle enthusiasm Armenians
Dark and rough eyebrows
Ancient Greek statue-like silhouette
Impressed me
The slogan of the demonstrators
The bloody massacre of the Turkish Empire in 1915
Wandering in my dream
I can only leave it with Dilijan City before I left
It has always a place for writers to put their dreams

Looking Through The Water

Last night
After the bird flew away
Seemed there to see the grief of a breaking heart
Different from the past day
No longer waiting for the first sunshine this morning
Keep the window open
Keep the window
Open all the way

last night
After the bird flew away
I
Became blind up to now
That lake scenery outside the window
No need to wait for the first sunshine this morning
That happily married couple on that boat
Keep the paddles
Rowing

That creek
Slowly flowing into the lake
With footsteps so light and can't be lighter
No any intention to bother
The bird that has flown away
and
That happily married couple on the boat
Like a lily among thorns
Until I closed
My window

Where Should The Youth Dreams Go?

Mountains towering and thick
Vast and deep water flowing around the valley
The past just In front of my mind has not disappeared
In the baggage
Loaded the earnest exhortations of my parents
My chest is crammed into a blah poem
A poetry
With where the youth dreams go
Ignorant! Ignorant! Ignorant! Ignorant! Ignorant! Ignorant!
Ignorant!

For endure great hardships in pioneer work
Raise the whip of the right hand
When is the partner's footsteps become so fast?
Sharp eyes
Lips closed without saying a word
The sound of condemning loud and heavy
Bigfoot
This growth arena couldn't bear it
Clatter! Clatter! Clatter! Clatter! Clatter! Clatter! Clatter!

The road ahead is so rampant
Watch out for every turn
The load on the chest will only be heavier and never be
alleviated.
Firm my mind
Past memories like a burst of smoke
Can't change everything in the future will come true soon
Growing up
Real life in exchange for a dream
Yeah! Yeah! Yeah! Yeah! Yeah! Yeah! Yeah!

Tzemin Ition Tsai

Shareef Abdur Rasheed

Shareef Abdur Rasheed

Shareef Abdur-Rasheed, AKA Zakir Flo was born and raised in Brooklyn, New York. His education includes Brooklyn College, Suffolk County Community College and Makkah, Saudi Arabia. He is a Veteran of the Viet Nam era, where in 1969 he reverted to his now reverently embraced Islamic Faith. He is very active in the Islamic community and beyond with his teachings, activism and his humanity.

Shareef's spiritual expression comes through the persona of "Zakir Flo" . Zakir is Arabic for "To remind". Never silent, Shareef Abdur-Rasheed is always dropping science, love, consciousness and signs of the time in rhyme.

Shareef is the Patriarch of the Abdur-Rasheed Family with 9 Children (6 Sons and 3 Daughters) and 41 Grandchildren (24 Boys and 17 Girls).

For more information about Shareef, visit his personal FaceBook Page at :

https://www.facebook.com/shareef.abdurrasheed1
https://zakirflo.wordpress.com

gateway/barrier

Caucasus
Georgia, Armenia,
Azerbaijan, Russia
extending to Turkey,
Iran, Abkhazia, Artsakh
Autonomous
Russia, Chechnya,
Dagestan, Ingushetia,
etc.
between the Black Sea,
Caspian Sea
see the Caucasus
Mountain range
Gateway/ barrier
between east, west,
eastern Europe, western Asia
peak of Mt. Elbrus 18,510 ft.
highest mountain in Europe
stands guard, bears witness
amazing mix of humanity
diversity
Indo-European, Turkic, Kartvelian
tongues
northeast, northwest indigenous
Russian in the northeast tip
Muslims, Jews, Christians
signs of humanity 2.8 million
years ago, in Georgia
multiple invasions
Christian dominance gave way
to Arab, Turk conquest
brought Islam

later Russian invasion
brought genocide
gold, alunite, chromium, copper,
iron ore, mercury etc. minerally
rich, culturally rich,
human mix rich
Caucasus rich, historically
noteworthy

food4thought = education

bloodlust

----

fitnah, fitnah, fitnah
mischief, trouble, test
all over the earth,
Carnage (Bloodletting),
Murder, homicide
senseless, brutal,
bloodlust orgy
godless, feigning godly
not hardly
took creator out the equation
kill for the sin-sation
blood spill is recreation
no magic pill to relieve damnation
only divine mercy will reverse the
curse heaped on a nation
by way of constant ungodly
forbidden participation
pray for the souls of the creation
to receive guidance, obey revelation
rehearse the verse
relieve the curse
but for now, conditions in deterioration
even though what seems to be
isn't it exactly?
more like criminal collusion
to hide in plain sight,
create an illusion,
keep the people
in state of confusion
establish wrong over right
plot to carry out devil's plight
but in spite

Allah's(swt) plan in full effect
day ' n ' night
look at man
something he don't
fully understand
man plots ' n ' plans
Allah(swt) has the best plan
be patient and pray for mankind
and the day when all this will
cease to exist, cease ' n ' desist
pass away from memory

food4thought = education

snakes
----

as they slither
in the grass
no matter how they try to fake
with the phony postures they
take
like putting lipstick on a pig
you dig?
a snake is a snake is a snake
just like the pit bulls folks get
for protection, intimidation
not just a pet
are snakes
with guns 'n' badges
or military uniforms dem wear
and even riot gear
become the norm
dem hide behind
come down on people already
in social/economic bind
with evil intent they're sent to
discourage, contain dissent
in their minds dem find dem
not to be
same as the people
they're sworn to serve, protect
instead there's
total disconnects
as far as the human aspect
they look at the faces and don't
see themselves as they do
with the images they relate to
which love ' n ' compassion

equate to
instead it's easy for them
to disrespect, feel hate
fueled by evil arrogance
mindless ignorance
it's bias dem create
that view me and you as
something other
rather than sisters, brothers
members of the human race
in your mind do you find
anything meaner that matches
the demeanor of a
cold blooded snake
especially if it's produced
and sponsored by the state?

food4thought = education

Shareef Abdur Rasheed

Kimberly Burnham

Find yourself in the pattern. As a 28-year-old photographer, Kimberly Burnham appreciated beauty. Then an ophthalmologist diagnosed her with a genetic eye condition saying, "Consider life, if you become blind." She discovered a healing path with insight, magnificence, and vision. Today, 33 years later, a poet and neurosciences expert with a PhD in Integrative Medicine, Kimberly's life mission is to change the global face of brain health. Using health coaching, Reiki, Matrix Energetics, craniosacral therapy, acupressure, and energy medicine, she supports people in their healing from brain, nervous system, and chronic pain issues. As managing editor of Inner Child Magazine, Kimberly's 2019 project is peace, language, and visionary poetry with her recently published book, *Awakenings: Peace Dictionary, Language and the Mind, a Daily Brain Health Program.*

http://www.NerveWhisperer.Solutions
https://www.linkedin.com/in/kimberlyburnham

The Peace of Self-Agreement

Two words in Lak
a Nakh-Dagestanian language
of Russia and the Northeast Caucasus
give a hint of how we feel
when we do what is right
for us

"Cuppa b-aq'-awu" and "curda d-aq'-awu"
from "aq'in" to be in agreement with someone
the words mean peace with oneself
self-agree or agreement
as if when we do what we agree
to ourselves is right
we are at peace

We can argue
you and I about what is right
for me for you
for the world
but in my heart I know what is right for me
and doing that
brings peace to me
to you and the world

Kazakhstan Expectations

Everywhere children are expected
to be strong and hope for fame
the Central Asian republic of Kazakhstan
finds peace "Бейбітшілік" or "bejbetsilik"
and love for children
every family wants a boy
born to be a defender of the clan
at war
to resemble famous noble people
or poets in the times of peace
as the land stretches
from the Caspian Sea in the East
to the Altai Mountains and China in the West
fighters and poets grow into men

The Circassian Heart at Rest

Peace or "гупсэху" in Adyghe
a Northwest Caucasus language
is two words
heart and rest
means two feelings
peace and comfortable

"Унэ гупсэф" is a comfortable house
where our heart can rest
we can find inner peace
as we travel and visit
where a Circassian greeting holds great import

"Iуэхум япэр фIэхъусщ"
"greetings precede all"
a token of peace
an implied welcome
an invitation to one's home
visitors and strangers consider salutatory words
a godsend
a promise of plentiful food and cozy lodgings
among friends

Elizabeth E. Castillo

Elizabeth Esguerra Castillo

Elizabeth Esguerra Castillo is a multi-awarded and an Internationally-Published Contemporary Author/Poet and a Professional Writer / Creative Writer / Feature Writer / Journalist / Travel Writer from the Philippines. She has 2 published books, "Seasons of Emotions" (UK) and "Inner Reflections of the Muse", (USA). Elizabeth is also a co-author to more than 60 international anthologies in the USA, Canada, UK, Romania, India. She is a Contributing Editor of Inner Child Magazine, USA and an Advisory Board Member of Reflection Magazine, an international literary magazine. She is a member of the American Authors Association (AAA) and PEN International.

Web links:

Facebook Fan Page

https://free.facebook.com/ElizabethEsguerraCastillo

Google Plus

https://plus.google.com/u/0/+ElizabethCastillo

The Kurds

Along the rugged terrain-
Of the Zagros Mountains
There they dwell,
The Land of the Kurds
Roaming the desert highway, night and day,
Nomadic people of the "Mesopotamian Plains"
Eclectic tribes led by their "aga"
Whose words are firm like the "sheik",
In Turkey, they are called the "Mountain Turks"
Ethnic people leading struggling lives
But made them tough and brave.

Signs

signs coming from the heavens,
asking God to have mercy on them
cries of a svelte, wretched soul-
echoes through the dark night like a trumpet
like the rhythms of jazz, a lone saxophone,
dribbling through the ears of one's beloved.

symbols likened to hands-
pointing to the right direction, coming out of nowhere,
a new frontier, where man embraces his tomorrow
some just stare-
and keep wandering around in circles
while the others enter doors of new horizons.
my beautiful butterfly-
the one that brought the sun to my garden.

metamorphosis-
the end to all sufferings
what everyone awaits
for

the end of my old life-
going peacefully
traversing the road to
eternity.

I love the captivating rainbow
and I would rather feast my eyes on its splendor
enchanting hues just like the changing seasons
of one's life-
a sign of hope of new things to come
I love you…

Road

She traveled to and fro-
Driving her old sedan
As I stare
Out of my window-
Fancy
Her red gown.
Picking up the pieces,
Fragments of memories
And things left undone,
She questioned God
Why was her road
An uneven one.
I loved the path I trekked-
Like a lover shows her affection for the beloved
Every now and then, I write in my diary-
My roller coaster ride,
Share to the universe moments of grief
And times of utter happiness.
A blue robin perched on a fragile branch
Fixed its eyes on the road-
I read its mind and I knew
How it longed to escape the place,
Its heart desired to awaken from this dream
And for its spirit to just fly away.

Joe
Paire

Joe Paire

Joseph L Paire' aka Joe DaVerbal Minddancer . . .
is a quiet man, born in a time where civil liberties
were a walk on thin ice. He's been a victim of his
own shyness often sidelined in his own quest for
love. He became the observer, charting life's path.
Taking note of the why, people do what they do. His
writings oft times strike a cord with the
dormant strings of the reader. His pen the rosined
bow drawn across the mind. He comes full-frontal
or in the subtlest way, always expressing in a way
that stimulate the senses.

www.facebook.com/joe.minddancer

Where Am I?

How do you remember history?
Do imaging warring factions wielding armor and their
captives
Do you admire the attire and inspire to be king
Or a trader for your neighbors bringing goods from across
the sea
Maybe it's the mountains those beautiful mountains
or the constant interference from other ruling governments
Caucasus, Caucasians did you immediately think
persuasion, this nation is quite different
Yet there is no difference
We all get influence from the love of diversity
Let me ask you this, is any man worry free?
conflict in the north south and surrounding borders
When will I be able to describe a place without war
So much culture so many languages it's a pity
The greed of man can't handle it
Peasants and overlords Present tense and oh my lord
They're still fighting, when a place so inviting
Is hidden in blood
They can say the same thing when they write about us
Where am I?
I'm in between dreams of seeing the world free

Night Porch

I caught the moons reflection in an amber sphere
I saw stars by a candle jars flame which has long gone out
stinking incense makes me homesick
Yet the pungency is attractive
Wild cacti grow and a broken bird house missed its guest
Don't protest the summer
Midnight slumber is often cooled at the right time
My pen and I start to write time
I write my vision through passers by
Memories don't serve me well
I frown when the sound strikes a chord
Having made it before I love new leaves
New trees new roots and the Night porch calls again
A harlequin of seashells so thin they chime in the wind
Hung by hemp string, sung by history
A world full of mystery if you make it so
Storyteller from the look of a jazz affair
The crack at your feet and I'll paint your drama
The turning leaves the turning leaves one hundred degrees
Sweat begins the pour no summer breeze in cramped
quarters or camp orders
I was just looking down at the likes of a soldier
The night holds you with its sounds
Egrets and wild turkey brass stars and quarter moons
Ah, but at twelve noon when shadows shift
I see the most beautiful land, it's called anywhere.

Smile On The Face

In the case of Propaganda, what is it? so let's visit.
The topic seems anthropic, if you look at it head on
The backward years reappear and wedge on
Smile on the face through obvious distaste
Man, your data base is spot on
Don't believe the hype, the crew, the news
The few who knew that smile was a ruse
Pamphlets, those gaudy pamphlets
The ladies' hand them out on entrance
Win this, when these displays get made
We're awe struck, then we are stuck on Kool-Aid
Smile on the face of early explores
Defeat the culture with negative stereo, type right.
Write onto the pages to sell this or that
Fib or fact, how do you sell your point
Endorsing a folly, bet you bout got it now
Bet you by golly wow
Bet you by tickets for a show that caught your eye
Propaganda, Smile on the face, same thing,
if the brain tries to sway you from believing a thing
Believe in a King, not a bare-naked emperor
Who won't wear a thing?
Smile in the face won't bare the pain of us
We're taught the vain in us
Who sought the vain in us, it's so harrowing?
When heroin does the same thing
It blinds the brain, be careful what you listen to
Listen through the thicket
I bet you thought I was going to say
Fortunately, I just wasn't taught that way
Comedy and Drama who writes the better comma
I mean, to give you pause.

hülya

n.

yilmaz

A retired Liberal Arts professor, hülya n. yılmaz [sic] is Co-Chair and Director of Editing Services at Inner Child Press International, and a literary translator. Her poetry has been published in an excess of sixty anthologies of global endeavors. Two of her poems are permanently installed in *TelePoem Booth*, a nation-wide public art exhibition in the U.S. She has shared her work in Kosovo, Canada, Jordan and Tunisia. hülya has been honored with a 2018 WIN Award of British Colombia, Canada. She is presently working on three poetry books and a short-story collection. hülya finds it vital for everyone to understand a deeper sense of self and writes creatively to attain a comprehensive awareness for and development of our humanity.

hülya n. yılmaz, Ph.D.

Writing Web Site
hulyanyilmaz.com

Editing Web Site
hulyasfreelancing.com

Ciscaucasia

with a sweeping gesture of the tongue,
i put the globe in the same sack
all the different regions, that is
all the different countries, that is
all the different languages, that is

a wishful thinking

behind my one-color glasses
the shade of oneness
the hue of unity within humanity

or . . .

could it be
that i am under the influence
of my own existence
as a thing of some substance?

what do i know?

regardless . . .

Ciscaucasia,
you are the closest
to that precious place
where i took my first breath
i was told, my father's family
had migrated from your mountain range
Dad was always proud
of their Russian Samovar

my oldest cousin, father-side,
named his two children
after you

behind my one-color glasses
the color of oneness
of unity within humanity

still . . .

what do i know?

Dagestan

as my childhood memories fade away
a few resilient ones seem determined to stay
one of them is a somber song to the mountains
where people, in marches, are forced to sway
there is heavy talk of many a smoke,
nothing short of a fatal stroke
yet the people march on
their voices, eventually,
turning into a whisper
then, barely there . . .

Dagestan,
what have you witnessed?

Azerbaycan

one of the many republics you were,

that much i know

the countless atrocities

you had to undergo

rarely don our books of your history

we'd much rather not look, you see,

for our image in the mirror

is as ugly as can be

not our first . . .

Teresa E. Gallion

Teresa E. Gallion

Teresa E. Gallion was born in Shreveport, Louisiana and moved to Illinois at the age of 15. She completed her undergraduate training at the University of Illinois Chicago and received her master's degree in Psychology from Bowling Green State University in Ohio. She retired from New Mexico state government in 2012.

She moved to New Mexico in 1987. While writing sporadically for many years, in 1998 she started reading her work in the local Albuquerque poetry community. She has been a featured reader at local coffee houses, bookstores, art galleries, museums, libraries, Outpost Performance Space, the Route 66 Festival in 2001 and the State of Oklahoma's Poetry Festival in Cheyenne, Oklahoma in 2004. She occasionally hosts an open mic.

Teresa's work is published in numerous Journals and anthologies. She has two CDs: *On the Wings of the Wind* and *Poems from Chasing Light*. She has published three books: *Walking Sacred Ground, Contemplation in the High Desert* and *Chasing Light*.

Chasing Light was a finalist in the 2013 New Mexico/Arizona Book Awards.

The surreal high desert landscape and her personal spiritual journey influence the writing of this Albuquerque poet. When she is not writing, she is committed to hiking the enchanted landscapes of New Mexico. You may preview her work at

http://bit.ly/1aIVPNq or *http://bit.ly/13IMLGh*

Not Complicated

The countries and people of Caucasus
are complicated. What is not is the epic
grandeur of the Caucasus Mountains
nestled between the Black Sea and the
Caspian Sea.

Georgia, Armenia, and Azerbaijan
make claims to this magnificent
landmass boasting the highest
mountain in Europe, Mount Elbrus.

Despite the violent history that
is common amongst all human
species across planet earth,
the mountains still call us home
to sit with nature.

Old Wind

Come to me old wind.
Shout the wisdom you bring.
I am here today ready
to assimilate your words.

I heard you scream,
you are blessed.
The flutter of your lips
always declare the truth.

My chest pumps joy.
I breathe in gratitude
sitting under the cottonwood
in a little piece of heaven.

A testament to the flow
of blessings in my life.
If I dare complain,
slap me hard and fast.

Forest Binding

On the path is a forest
engulfed in flames of silence
waiting to enfold you
in a divine embrace.

Dirt clings to the contour
of your boots as your feet
softly touch the earth.

The wind's gentle whisper
is music to your ears.
Brings you to your knees
unable to hold the rapture
that binds you to the forest.

Ashok K. Bhargava

Ashok Bhargava is a poet, writer, community activist, public speaker, management consultant and a keen photographer. Based in Vancouver, he has published several collections of his poems: Riding the Tide, Mirror of Dreams, A Kernel of Truth, Skipping Stones, Half Open Door and Lost in the Morning Calm. His poetry has been published in various literary magazines and anthologies.

Ashok is a Poet Laureate and poet ambassador to Japan, Korea and India. He is founder of WIN: Writers International Network Canada. Its main objective is to inspire, encourage, promote and recognize writers of diverse genres, artists and community leaders. He has received many accolades including Nehru Humanitarian Award for his leadership of Writers International Network Canada, Poets without Borders Peace Award for his journeys across the globe to celebrate peace and to create alliances with poets, and Kalidasa Award for creative writings.

Defying Realism

I look around
thinking where are the Caucasus
and a handful of countries
I've known
only to find
all whites are now Caucasians.

I wonder
then what are the people from the Caucasus?
(If native Americans are Indians
Then what are the people from India?)

Is this another form of racism
to call ourselves what we are not,
to draw up boundaries
to feel safe as
a precondition for surviving.

Caucasus mountains stand
indifferent
as mystifying as a dream

- Caucasian, literally, refers to people native to the Caucasus, but it has become interchangeable with 'White' populations, most of whom trace their ancestry to Europe. I think that the people who use the term 'Caucasian' likely do not know where the Caucasus mountains are.
- Armenia, Azerbaijan, Georgia and parts of Caucasus conquered by Russia

Senses

Explore life
Discover love
Feel the vibration

Adore surroundings
Develop passion
Experience intimacy

Seek ecstasy
Ignite joy
Crave for a soul mate

If I were another I
You were other than you
The world still would be same

Remember
There are many ways
To hear, taste, touch, see and smell

Ashok K. Bhargava

Words

When a poem dawns on me
it shines it's light on me
beauty I hardly deserve.

Showering of words
pour down
delicately
l am drenched.

Swaying in elation
I forget the difference
between pain and healing
between light and dark
between faith and doubts
between promises
our bodies make
and the ones
they keep.

Caroline 'Ceri Naz' Nazareno

Carolin 'Ceri' Nazareno

Caroline Nazareno-Gabis a.k.a. Ceri Naz, born in Anda, Pangasinan known as a 'poet of peace and friendship', is a multi-awarded poet, journalist, editor, publicist, linguist, educator, and women's advocate.

Graduated cum laude with the degree of Bachelor of Elementary Education, specialized in General Science at Pangasinan State University. Ceri have been a voracious researcher in various arts, science and literature. She volunteered in Richmond Multicultural Concerns Society, TELUS World Science, Vancouver Art Gallery, and Vancouver Aquarium.

She was privileged to be chosen as one of the Directors of Writers Capital International Foundation (WCIF), Member of the Poetry Posse, one of the Board of Directors of Galaktika ATUNIS Magazine based in Albania; the World Poetry Canada and International Director to Philippines; Global Citizen's Initiatives Member, Association for Women's rights in Development (AWID) and Anacbanua. She has been a 4th Placer in World Union of Poets Poetry Prize 2016, Writers International Network-Canada ''Amazing Poet 2015'', The Frang Bardhi Literary Prize 2014 (Albania), the sair-gazeteci or Poet-Journalist Award 2014 (Tuzla, Istanbul, Turkey) and World Poetry Empowered Poet 2013 (Vancouver, Canada).

Two refrains

we came from different directions
you were the *nefesh*
i am the *neshuma*
but we believed
we can merge as one
like rainmakers
dancing amidst the fields
of wonderment,
our endless refrain.

 we meet with open windows
both in nostalgic stares
we prance in joy and sorrows
exchange steps from our own battles,
with one purpose: continue searching
the meaning of tomorrow,
as we cross mountains
and ebbing the tides.

Whisper of Hope

c'est la vie…
the towering boulders,
the summit to dream
invited me again
"go where you feel most alive"

lush of greens
earth reminds beautiful start
reinvigorating cadence
new dreams, new beginnings
where the sky of hope
says, ''go where your heart takes you''

spring's secret lullaby

waiting for the pearly morn

cascading with infinite dew drops

crystalline symphonies on the clouds

whispering silver charming flames

a song bird singing merry silhouettes

in the majestic hours of spring

with you by my side is a dream

like secrets lulling mellow chants

while dancing to life's windmills of chance

Swapna Behera

Swapna Behera is a bilingual contemporary poet, author, translator and editor from Odisha, India .She was a teacher from 1984 to 2015 . Her stories, poems and articles are widely published in National and International journals, and ezines, and are translated into different national and International languages. She has penned four books. She was conferred upon the Prestigious International Poesis Award of Honor at the 2nd Bharat Award for Literature as Jury in 2015, The Enchanting Muse Award in India World Poetree Festival 2017, World Icon of Peace Award in 2017, and the Pentasi B World Fellow Poet in 2017.. She is the recipient of Gold Cross Of Wisdom Award ,the medal for The Best Teachers of the World from World Union of Poets in 2018, and The LIfe time Achievement Award ,The Best Planner Award, The Sahitya Shiromani Award, ATAL BiHARI BAJPAYEE AWARD 2018, Ambassador De Literature Award 2018 .She is the Ambassador of Humanity by Hafrikan Prince Art World Africa 2018 and an official member of World Nation's Writers Union ,Kazakhstan2018. At present she is the manager at Large, Planner and Columnist of The Literati, the administrator of several poetic groups ,the member of the Special Council of Five of World Union of Poets and the Cultural Ambassador of Inner Child Press U.S.

The Address of The Heaven

here is the Heaven
between the Black sea
and Caspian sea
the hamlets
of the Caucasians
the migratory birds
sparkling moon
in sync with all invisible directions
blue eyes , classic lips
tall damsels dancing
their skirts flutter with the tune of the
bagpipers
where the earth is ploughed
after the shower
the footsteps codify
rhyme and rhythm
ethnic celebration
of fresh air
cater the catalogue of colours
and dialogue of honours
Heavenly poetry written by trees
sprinkle fragrance of tulips
exactly where
the drumbeats
merge with heartbeats
the Heaven is here
and here ....

Each Answer is Hash Tagged

each answer is hash tagged
with
a popping question,
a dream;
a palette,
an ascend
a goose bump
a lustrous reception
a graffiti of butterflies
a prayer,
a promise,
a verse,
a pause ,
drops of tears
and
the last word of a promising Anthem.

each answer
is
a combination and permutation
a dot in a circle and a circle in a dot
a drop in the ocean and an ocean in the drop
a road map from eyes to alphabets
a closed chapter of references
and inferences .

each answer speaks
"hey ! I am coming back after just a short break .
till then best wishes ......"

Swapna Behera

Once again

Once again
democracy will march
 on the curved village roads
farmers will hoist the green flag
rivers will twist and bend
 to satisfy all
the air ,water and soil will be fresh
as the virgin eyes of a new born
irrespective of every time zone and latitudes

once again
the bangle seller
will sell in the market
the soldiers will be back
after a peace treaty

once again
people will celebrate truth ;
 blindfolded statues
will be removed from the courts

once again
each blind child will get the retina
from you or me
 smile will replace anger

once again ;
nature will teach us love ....

Albert 'Infinite' Carrasco

Albert 'Infinite' Carassco

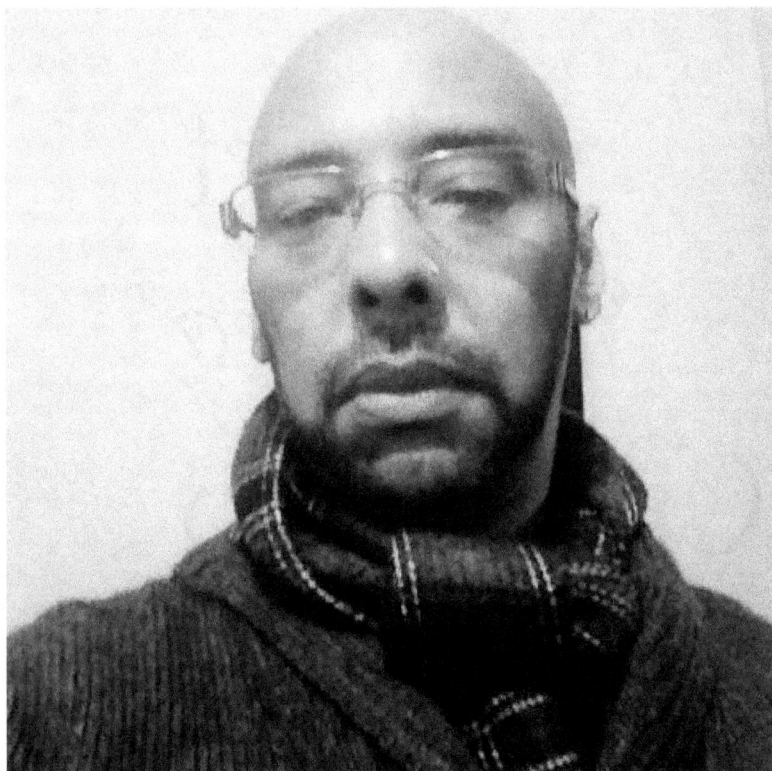

I'm a project life philanthropist, I speak about the non ethical treatment of poor ghetto people. Why? My family was their equal, my great grandmother and great grandfather was poor, my grandmother and grandfather, my mother and father, poverty to my family was a sequel, a traditional Inheritance of the subliminal. I paid attention to the decades of regression, i tried to make change, but when I came to the fork in the road and looked at the signs that read wrong < > right, I chose the left, the wrong direction, because of street life interactions a lot around me met death or incarceration. I failed myself and others. I regret my decisions, I can't reincarnate dead men, but I can give written visions in laymens. I'm back at that fork in the road, instead of it saying wrong or right, I changed it, now it says dead men < > life.

Infinite poetry @lulu.com

Alcarrasco2 on YouTube

Infinite the poet on reverbnation

Infinite Poetry

http://www.lulu.com/us/en/shop/al-infinite-carrasco/infinite-poetry/paperback/product-21040240.html

Caucasus

Between the Caspian and Black Sea,
Is home to Armenia, Azerbaijan, Georgia and Russia,
The Caucasus mountains are a barrier between Europe and
Western Asia.
Abkhazo-Adyghian, Nakho-Dagestanian and kartvelian,
are the indigenous languages spoken by the Caucasian.
Ciscaucasus is the north and Transcaucasus is the south,
Separated by the lower and greater mountain ranges.
Mt Elbrus is so tall,
Petroglyphs on rock in Gobustan look like an artist
personal wall.
This land was home to early man,
Fossils from a million years ago was found by an
archeologist hand.
Cathedrals, Palaces, Mosques, Forts and mausoleums are
all historical.

Saw it all

Infinite is a poet straight out the BX, I lived my genre in Castle hill, that's where I watched hustlers pop guns and stack funds from drug sales made in or around the projects. I saw some blow and move, I've seen some try to blow but lose and I've heard guns blow and saw some bleeding out while their parents begged them to move. Poverty had me willing to take chances. I Dreamt of being like the ones that made it, I knew getting in wouldn't mean I'll win, I could lose after trying or be the one snug in a casket while everyone is crying. I was hungry so I took the first opportunity offered to make money. I was out there with my kin, we had the same plight, same view but different windows when we watched hustlers hustle and broad day or late night gunfights. we stood back to back trying to get our pockets right. We got it all, cash, cars, jewelry. Money power respect and anytime anywhere pussy. We lived the life. I mean we came up fast, red was the brand, but because of the chefs hand it didn't matter the color, we could ROY G BIV the ave and multiply math, our material was stronger. It's wasn't all glitz and glamor. One dead. Two dead. Ten dead. When we was young watching and playing the game, we heard the shots and saw the money, but those sights and sounds didn't come with the feeling of hurt and pain, when you're living the life.. those emotions are gained.

Dementia

Bendicion. Y dios de bendiga. Saying that is the first thing I say every time I see her. I'll pucker up and give her a kiss on her forehead while she's sitting in her chair or laying in her bed. I can see her face light up with joy, like ahhh there's my boy. How's your mother and brothers? They're fine. How's the kids? They're fine too. Gracias a dios. I make sure she took a shower and is dressed properly. I look in the closet and drawers to make sure she has all her property, then grab her remote to put on her favorite Spanish channel on TV. Apágalo! do you think electricity is free? She thinks the nursing home is home. She's fed, but not our traditional food so I bring rice, beans, baked chicken, bistec, carne guisada, or soup and her favorite...Spanish coffee with a little bit of milk and sugar, which always puts her in a relaxed mood. Sometimes she eats on her own and others I feed her. I can sit with her and talk for an hour. It'll be a great conversation between grandma and grandson. Some days are better than others. What I mean is, sometimes she's confused and forgetful. Bendicion grandma. I give her her kiss and I'll hear, Oh you know me? Thank you for the kiss. As if I'm a nice stranger. It's me Albert, Albert? My daughters son? No you're not Albert, where's your mother? In Florida. Florida? Ah bueno. My sister Emilia came to see me yesterday. (It blows my mind because her sister died more than a decade ago, by no means will I let her know that, so I run with it.) Emilia came? that's great. How is she? She looks good and young. Why are you here? I came to see you. Why? To make sure you're okay. I'm just fine. I brought you food. Ay no, I'm full. I'll ask the nurses if she ate, they'll say no, she hasn't eaten because she's waiting for you to bring her food. I'm offering her the food but to her I'm not me at that moment. Two minutes later she's holding my hand telling me how much I'm missed. It's hard, but I keep my composure wishing there was no such thing as dementia.

Eliza
Segiet

After earning a Master's Degree in Philosophy at the Jagiellonian University in Krakaw, Poland, Eliza Segiet proceeded with her post-graduate studies in the fields of Cultural Knowledge, Penal Revenue and Economic Criminal Law, Arts and Literature and Film and Television Production in the Polish city, Lodz.

With specific regard to her creative writings, the author describes herself as being torn in her passion for engaging in two literary genres: Poetry and Drama. A similar dichotomy from within is reflected on Segiet's own words about her true nature: She likes to look at the clouds, but she keeps both of her feet set firmly on the ground.

The author describes her worldview as being in harmony with that of Arthur Schopenhauer: "Ordinary people merely think how they shall 'spend' their time; a man of talent tries to 'use' it".

Forever
In memory of Those who stayed there

For the love of the mountains
they go to places hard to reach
– to make dreams come true:

to be above the clouds,
to experience differently,
to see more.

For the love of the mountains
– they take risk.
Some of them reach
inhospitable summits.
Thirsty for adventures,
they are still trying.

Kazbek, Elbrus
are not just their plans
– they are the goals.

An order
of desires and certainty.
Despite everything, it's worth it.
The language of time
will show who has arrived
and who has not managed.

For the love of the mountains
they return

or they stay forever.

translated by Artur Komoter

New Opening

She stopped planning,
waiting and dreaming.
Her monotonous time,
it became overwhelming.

In the evenings she whispered:
– *No future anymore.*
Time to die?

Everything apart from her?

It is not too late yet
to do something,
to get to know a fraction
of the world's secrets.

Every day is a new opening
– not a time to shut the longings
in unaccomplishment.

In the beginning she chose Georgia.
Delighted with the beauty of
Tbilisi, Batumi, Poti
– she breathed more fully.

She already knew that
the wind of her strength
will become the
previously unattainable goals.

translated by Artur Komoter

Eliza Segiet

Time of Solstice

Time of solstice – a time of transition,
looking differently,
not turning back.
Attempt at the end – an attempt at the beginning.

How to begin?

The moon is like it was,
the sun rises and sets.
Only I see it differently –
the irreversible progression of life,
the maturity of the panorama of
the fossils of memories
drawn into my time.

1] My submission is my original work, and no part has
been copied from any other work.
I own all rights in my submission. There is no need to get
permission for publication.

2] I don't expect the payment for the publication.

translated by Artur Komoter

William S.

Peters Sr.

Bill's writing career spans a period of over 50 years. Being first Published in 1972, Bill has since went on to Author in excess of 40 additional Volumes of Poetry, Short Stories, etc., expressing his thoughts on matters of the Heart, Spirit, Consciousness and Humanity. His primary focus is that of Love, Peace and Understanding!

Bill says . . .

I have always likened Life to that of a Garden. So, for me, Life is simply about the Seeds we Sow and Nourish. All things we "Think and Do", will "Be" Cause and eventually manifest itself to being an "Effect" within our own personal "Existences" and "Experiences" . . . whether it be Fruit, Flowers, Weeds or Barren Landscapes! Bill highly regards the Fruits of his Labor and wishes that everyone would thus go on to plant "Lovely" Seeds on "Good Ground" in their own Gardens of Life!

to connect with Bill, he is all things Inner Child

www.iaminnerchild.com

Personal Web Site

www.iamjustbill.com

Caucuses

From the mountains
And the caves
Came one
Who sought to enslave
The world

Hunters Gatherers
Conquerors, Wanderers
With a wonder
That consumed
The known world
And other civilizations
That had no correlation
To the equation
We call . . . humanity

Assimilators
Of those
Who were not of . . .
A land of many languages,
Culture
And ways of life

They endured the harshness
Of the unfriendly mountainous region
And though equal
Disbanded
Amongst themselves

From this was borne . . .
Colonialism,
Imperialism,
Capitalism

And other 'isms'
Were given birth
Upon the earth
That man to this day
Must endure

Just like Little Bo Peep

Lying face down in the pillow
Waiting for the torrid dreams
And horrid screams
To arrive
And drive me
Over the edge

Nightmares were my best friends
I could depend upon them
To always be there ....
By day at times,
By night all times

Shhhhh...
I hear someone coming,
Twigs being broken
Upon the forest floor,
The moon filtering through
The canopy of fright,
Looming blooming
Incantations spoken
Into my broken-mess
Blessing me
With fears
I must learn to face

Imagination...
Out of control
Giving cause for the tension
In the center sphere
Of my glutemous maximus
Where my apprehension

Settles and collects
To meddle with suspect
About my un at ease
Which I can only appease
With another painkiller

Which disturbs me most,
Is it my sciatica
Or this brain stuff
That fluffs up
My weariness
Blinding me
From the light,
Yet reminding me
Of the enduring night
I suffer

I suffocate myself
With expectations
Of the Joy in the morning
That never seems to arrive
At the dawning
Of my 1st light
And I wonder
Just how alive
Am I

I do strive though my friend,
But even I question
To what end,
For the blending ... in
The mending sin
Has not given leeway
To this evolving fix
Where I no longer have to pretend

To give a damn

Sam was a good ole boy,
But who was he really,
Was he anything
Like me?
As a matter of fact
Who is anyone
I ask, for truly,
We don't know 'Jack'
About why
We are attacked
At a spiritual level

I look through the
Beveled glass,
And everything is distorted
And here I am
Cohorting
With my conjured demons of verse
Attempting to expunge
The terseness
Of my trepidation

I long for a bit more
Of that euphoric ghost
That visits
Every now and then,
And perhaps,
Just perhaps
I can convince him
To sit a bit,
Stay a while
And have a meal
Just before now

When I lay my self down
Once more
To sleep
And count my sheep
Just like
Little Bo Peep

The Building

The Building
There was a time
That there was this building
That took presence and shape
In my horizon
As it loomed ominously,
Calling oft times
. . . my name

It was an empty sort of place
With no walls,
Just doors and windows ...
All open

Most of my waking consciousness
Was aware
Of this structure
That had come
To become
An integral part
Of all my thoughts

I began to house my dreams
In the ether
About it.
My desires for self and others,
And our world
Lived there too

Some times, that was enough . . .
But it truly wasn't

So ...
I began to erect walls
And adorn them
With my 'me-ness' ...
And expectations for
Whom I would allow
To cross my threshold

This structure,
This place
Where I stored
My inadequacies
Became a favorite place
For me to hang out,
Along with my
Excuses,
My delusions,
And my
Delicate,
Decrepit,
Dilapidated,
Self Deifying ...
Beliefs ....
.....
Call it conviction
If you will,
But 'Will'
Had naught to do
With it certainty.

In circumspective contemplative buffoonery
I considered and surmised
To my mild myopic surprise,
And I declaratively declared ...
"Whoa be me I said, I see

That is your purpose
O Building" ....
....
At that time,
The Building removed itself
From its illusory foundation
And approached me
And said ....
"Life's simple question is
What are you building?"

September
2019
Featured Poets

~ * ~

Elena Liliana Popescu

Gobinda Biswas

Iram Fatima 'Ashi'

Joseph S. Spence, Sr.

I FLY because I Can ... said the Dreamer to the world.

Elena Liliana Popescu

Elena Liliana Popescu (1948, Turnu Măgurele, Teleorman, Romania) is Doctor in Mathematics and Professor at the University of Bucharest, Romania. She is poet, translator and editor, member of the Writers' Union of Romania and the Romanian PEN Centre.

She has published more than 50 books of poetry and translations from English, Spanish. Her poems, translated into more than 20 languages, have been published in various volumes, anthologies in literary magazines in Albania, Argentina, Australia, Bangladesh, Bolivia, Brazil, Canada, Chile, Colombia, Cuba, El Salvador, Estonia, Germany, Hungary, India, Italy, Mexico, Mongolia, Nicaragua, Pakistan, Poland, Puerto Rico, Republic of Moldova, Romania, Serbia, Spain, Taiwan, Turkey, Uruguay, USA.

She has curated numerous poetry volumes, monographs and essays. She has published translations in literary magazines from the works of over one hundred authors. She has participated in several literary events abroad (Brazil, Chile, Cuba, France, Italy, Mexico, Spain, Nicaragua, Turkey, USA).

When you are found

The shore reigns in the ocean's freedom
Full darkness contains the light
Upon the still land, fear is the wave
that leaves in its wake the world to come.

Everything is nothing in seeking immortality
In this mute despair silence is the word.
Even unhappiness contains the happiness
when, humbled, you will leave this world.

Subdued illusion hides the truth
revealed only when you depart-
today the merely transitory
becomes eternal when you're found.

When everything is lost

The clock did not stop
but hours no longer show
on Time's dial,
which has come to a standstill, contemplating.

Perspective still works,
but objects are no longer clear
against the pure expanse
of unnamed Space.

Life has not ended but death
no longer looms at the horizon
waiting for someone to rise up
sometime, somewhere, in the land of oblivion...

Everything is as it used to be
though nothing has meaning
when lost in a timeless space,
in a spaceless time…

Elena Liliana Popescu

That instant

A few words, you told yourself,
just a few—and created
a story whose present
is yesterday by now, just as tomorrow
will be past for another story
left behind,
lost forever...

One word, you told yourself,
just one— and you are on your way
the unknown,
that unexpected step, free
to think of who you are and are not,
of that instant in which you can become
and be you.

English version by Adrian G Sahlean

Gobinda
Biswas

Gobinda Biswas is a poet who hails from West Bengal, India. He is an Assistant Teacher of English at Vivekanandanagar Vivekananda High School. He has published A book of 86 self - composed and original English poems namely 'The Sunny Poems' Published in May, 2016 and a book of 90 self-composed poems 'The Universal Poems'. His work has appeared in countless anthologies and magazines globally.

You can connect with him via FaceBook

https://www.facebook.com/profile.php?id=1000090298419
90

To my Olivia

O my Olivia, you live thousands of miles away
Beyond the rivers, near the seas in pleasure,
Always you dreamt the life of true abundance
Your dream is fulfilled, you live with treasure.

You taught me how to dream a good dream
Then I was really beside myself with joy,
Beside the river, 'neath the teak we whispered
Hands upon hands, eyes upon eyes, you were coy.

I took you as my Hero, I was Leander
So, I crossed the Hellespont but all in vain,
I was not the Edward-viii, O my Wally
He arrived, you caught hand and I'm in pain.

You were my Thisbe,I was your Paramus
Under the mull-berry tree we would sit for hours,
No whisper, no talking, we gazed at the rain-bow
Years have passed; alone I gaze and shed tears.

These are the paths, now I can clearly see
Smiling we are walking side by side,
This is the old Burma teak under whose feet
 Still in tears I'm rowing the canoe in hide.

The Soldier is Crying

I am a soldier, a really brave soldier
Always you think I have no finer feelings,
That I'm a machine like the cruel machine gun
Truly speaking I don't like bombings and firings.

Despite that I am going to the battle-field
To kill those imaginary enemies I don't know,
Who have done no harm to me at all
They're not my enemies, I can't help but rue.

On the contrary, I also might be killed in front
Those soldiers never wanted me to slay,
Thus either we, the soldiers kill or be killed
Not we but Mars triumphs on the Death Valley.

Now I am on way to the horrible war-front
Over there   are my wife with our little darling,
She rushed to me and began to wail loudly
My throat got chocked while I was weeping.

She was panicked that I would not come back
For too few would return from the bloody battle,
She was howling, 'Please, don't go to the front'
I took little child to arms and she began to rattle.

In 4001 B.C.

We are the humans of 4001 B.C.
While the world is really beautiful,
We suffer from three primal needs
But our social environment is so cool.

We are not divided by any border
For we have no so called country,
We have the whole of the earth
Where like air we are totally free.

We have no refugee problem
For we can migrate anywhere,
From our native land we've spread
Across the world, dear, O dear.

We don't know the so called religions
They kill humans even in 21st century,
We have no beliefs in imaginary gods
We do not write fabricated history.

Avoid all the complications of your minds
You're great grand-sons and grand-daughters,
We notice your miseries and get agonized
Abandon violence, live in peace and pleasures.

Iram
Fatima
'Ashi'

I am Iram Fatima 'Ashi'. I am nonresident Indian staying in Saudi Arabia. I was born and raised in India.

I pursued graduation and post graduation in English. I have been writing since the age of 13 in Hindi, Urdu and English. I am currently working as an Editor in chief of 'Reflection online magazine', **Editorial Executive Sub-Committee member of VIEW** (Print journal) and my creative work is part of 41 international anthologies, one poetry book and one novel. My articles, short stories and poems are published in Indian magazines and newspapers. Internationally, my work is published in Canada and US. I feel blessed on being honored by 'Aagman Gourav 2015, 2016 &2017' by Aagman group.

To witness nature from the height

In the lap of nature, a widely open view,
Beautiful to watch, welcoming with open arms,
Trapped in strange fascination, felt good with pride,
When I get a chance to witness, nature from the height.

Tiny moving creatures, a close look of flying birds,
Chilled airwaves are touching with wet clouds,
Climate and my mood, on its peak and delight,
When I get a chance to witness nature from the height.

I wish I could be a photographer to capture this moment,
Or I would be a painter to paint this splendor scenery,
A musician to compose a song, or a poet so that I can write,
When I get a chance to witness nature from the height.

I wish you could be here by my side, close by,
With this playful nature, absorbing all this exquisite,
I want to witness this beauty, while hugging you tight,
When I get a chance to witness nature from the height.

A Silence

A silence,
That screams with the creatures of the night,
Echoing through the dark path ways,
Dreads the soul of travelers, passing by
A silence,
An outcome of an extreme love,
A caring heart that always went unnoticed,
Anger, amidst the solitude
A silence,
An articulation, that bears no words,
A sword, slowly cutting into the insides,
A denied, unknown darkness growing within!

Iram Fatima 'Ashi'

The Abandoned Soul

My soul begs me for something,
Something lost in the tides of time,
I look back at their smiling faces,
Their eyes not even for once meeting mine

There's no sound,
But I can hear their laughter,
They won't even look at my face,
If only they could see how I feel!

I know no one would call me,
Nor take me by the hand,
For I have been condemned,
Set as an example for everyone to see!

I take a final look at the marks I left behind.
A feeling of nostalgia makes me cry,
I'm free, I tell myself as I begin to climb,
I am moving forward, my spirit shall sail on!

A new life awaits me,
There in the darkness of empty spaces,
Where no emotions tread by,
No memories to haunt my tortured mind!

Joseph S. Spence, Sr.

Joseph S. Spence, Sr., author of seven poetry books, invented, "Epulaeryu Poetry." His writings appeared nationally and internationally in forums such as: journals, anthologies, magazines, newspapers and the U. S. Army. He taught at Bryant and Stratton University, retired from the U.S. Army, and is a Goodwill Ambassador. He received many awards including: Literary Golden Badge 5/2019 (Oman), Poetry Gold Medal Honors 5/2019 (Africa), Noble Star for Literature 12/2018 (India). Poetry Ambassador Medal, Independent Poet Laureate, Who's Who in Poetry, and Editor's Choice Awards (USA); and Poetry Bard (UK). He has membership in various scholastic honor societies, and resides, USA.

Joseph S. Spence, Sr.

If We Must Die

Dedicated to the Natural Spirit of Claude McKay,
Jamaican and Harlem Renaissance Poet. September 15,
1889—May 22, 1948

Your words, "If we must die."
Created an indominable spirit, which inspired world leaders
to stand up. Fighting back against tyranny and oppression,
during World War II, when their backs where against the
wall, thus, awakening resiliency and buoyancy which saved
countries around the world.

Your words, "If we must die."
Created an indominable spirit, which joined hands together
to serve a noble cause for the betterment of humankind;
thus, bringing others together to sit around the table of
brotherhood, in the land of the free, and home of the brave.

Your words, "If we must die."
Created an indominable spirit, which saved many lives
from, anger and reprisal against each other, thus, resulting
in peace and prosperity, bringing about unity, calming
anxiety, tranquility, and a true quality of life.

Your words, "If we must die."
Created an indominable spirit, which allowed beautiful
songs to stimulate our souls with love. Radiating from the
magnificent choral voices of our children and
grandchildren. Immersing themselves in our great cultural
heritage of wisdom, knowledge, and understanding.

Your words, "If we must die."
Created an indominable spirit, which suppressed the agony
of an unscrupulous person ripping off our safety deposit
boxes, and cleaning out our bank accounts, while we are
resting in a home for the aged somewhere.

Alas, my brother, your words, "If we must die."
Created an indominable spirit of life, thus, letting us know,
that death will be after, and only after, our souls have
passed on the renaissance knowledge of life to all
humankind.

Like a shining star, gliding across the universe, from the
East to West. One which raises aspiring heads and beaming
eyes.

Opening up wondering minds, and joy filled hearts, thus,
leaving on the tongue of those who seek to reach for it…

Words of everlasting hope— "I wish!

Then, and only then, if we must die, only Heaven awaits
us!

Red Sea Historical—Persona Poem

Sitting here, in combat gear, time to spare
Your beautiful coral reefs relaxing minds many
Camping down at Sharm el Sheik
Touching your soft soothing surface at night
Looking royal with the—soft setting sun
You rocked, while I humanely hummed.

Kindness you extended to Darius of Persia
Even helped Alexander the Great
Your history included Augustus of Rome
Bonaparte was childish, claiming your captivity
Such natural spirit of nature; if only he knew
You were red, never intended being blue.

Sitting here my inquisitive right-hand gliding
Touching your slick and soothingly
Splashy soft surface—so stimulating!
Beholding your balmy and mystic spiritual soul
Sinking my hand below your naturally
Reddish curvy waves, your response—a ripple!

Moses, the Good Shepherd, had his ways
Spiritually, liberating Israel from Egypt
Opening your midst you allowed his passage
Such an Exodus, from Pharaoh pounding pursuit
Saving a nation—Yam Suph!
Working a natural miracle, natures special way.

One day, expect my return to relax with you
Without combat gear, weapons, nor bullets
Diving below your splashing surface

Where the spirit of medieval natural spices
Rests in the depth of your tectonic plates
Will be such a real rush for remembrance.

On the illustrious and illuminating coast of Eilat
There I will relax in a glass-bottom boat
Wondering, if your beauty will always be red
Until then, moisture Aqaba's Gulf
Quench Sinai's watery thirst, and as always:
Flow well—Red Sea!

Great Spirited Advocate--Nelson Mandela, Umtata, South Africa!

Nelson Mandela, crossed my spirited mind today, a visionary and legendary leader of equality, liberty, and unity; a man of honor and great fiber for his people!

He was a Greek God fighting for the—"Common man!" Displaying indomitable courage and lion-hearted temperament.

My spirit copiously read how he unlocked the chains off doors and chambers of darkness, containing humans as caged birds, without wings or a song.

His spirit displayed the personification of highest aspiration, showing such self-sacrifice and hailed by his people as, "Bafana, " their —"Great Stalwart!"

His true nature vehemently fought against apartheid as a freedom fighter on the frontier, leading the charge with formidable faith.

While imprisoned in South Africa: Spirited libertarians and people of goodwill worked diligently— "So feverously fighting for his freedom.

Organizing, boycotting, striking, singing, uplifting his name, and praying for the glorious day for all to see his release from traumatizing and rusting shackles of oppression

His spirit made, "Flowers of peace bloomed," without allowing solitude to change his attitude, break his relentless fortitude, or crushed his—"Great magnitude!"

Spiritedly chosen, "Father of the Nation," rising as a
powerful "Catalyst for Change," he enhanced liberty
and equality—"Fought for and obtained freedom for
his people!"

He was honored, with the World Prize for Peace, over
250 awards, honors, and many more citations of
elevation that anyone I have known.

Renowned for walking the walk and talking the talk,
with dignity, by nature he was —so mesmerizing and
sacrificing. "A leader like no other!"

Like a thunderous bolt from the heart and arms of
Zeus, he reached very far and wide, penetrating the
deepest depths and widest width!

Creating a devastating upheaval within the tectonic
plates of the bastions of racism, while liberating
those illegally confined in dark dungeons of
degradational abyss.

His was like a dolphin, swimming among deadly
sharks, with bodily dismembering teeth, while fighting
for others to obtain, liberty and equality.

His was like a salmon, swimming upstream to precious
breading grounds, while eagles, and big black bears,
waited with razor edge cutting sharp claws.

His was rays of the golden sun at dawn, illuminating
darkness, providing light to the world and opening
eyes so people would see the true light.

His was shining stars at night, twinkling great
majestical beauty; so immutably bright for the world,
inspiring hearts and minds to always shine!

As I read along, images of a great hero timely appeared, uplifting my mind, body, and soul with much joy and positive inspiration.

As one, who have impacted the world with lightening narrations! Illuminating the good life, shown through elation.

Standing up he firmly took my right hand, looked me in the eyes, gave me a big hug, a pat on the back, and said — "My Brother!"

Such sincerely! Now I know his legacy will be here to stay, every day, in a very special way, night or day, while others pray!

Remembering

our fallen soldiers of verse

Janet Perkins Caldwell

February 14, 1959 ~ September 20, 2016

Alan W. Jankowski

16 March 1961 ~ 10 March 2017

Coming
April 2020

The
World Healing, World Peace
International Poetry Symposium

Stay Tuned

for more information
intouch@innerchildpress.com

'building bridges of cultural understanding'
www.innerchildpress.com

Inner Child Press
News

Poetry Posse Members

We are so excited to share and announce a few of the current books, as well as the new and upcoming books of some of our Poetry Posse authors.

On the following pages we present to you ...

Jackie Davis Allen

Gail Weston Shazor

hülya n. yılmaz

Nizar Sartawi

Faleeha Hassan

Fahredin Shehu

Caroline 'Ceri' Nazareno

Eliza Segiet

William S. Peters, Sr.

Now Available at
www.innerchildpress.com

No Illusions

Through the Looking Glass

Jackie Davis Allen

Now Available at
www.innerchildpress.com

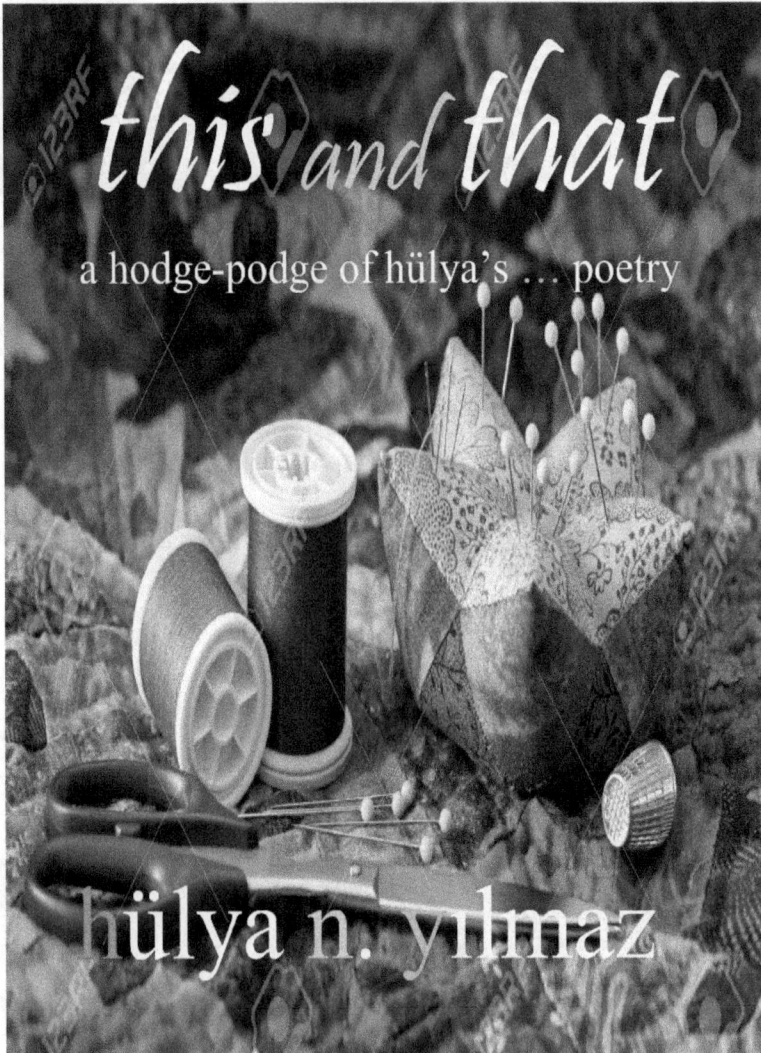

this and that

a hodge-podge of hülya's ... poetry

hülya n. yılmaz

Now Available at
www.innerchildpress.com

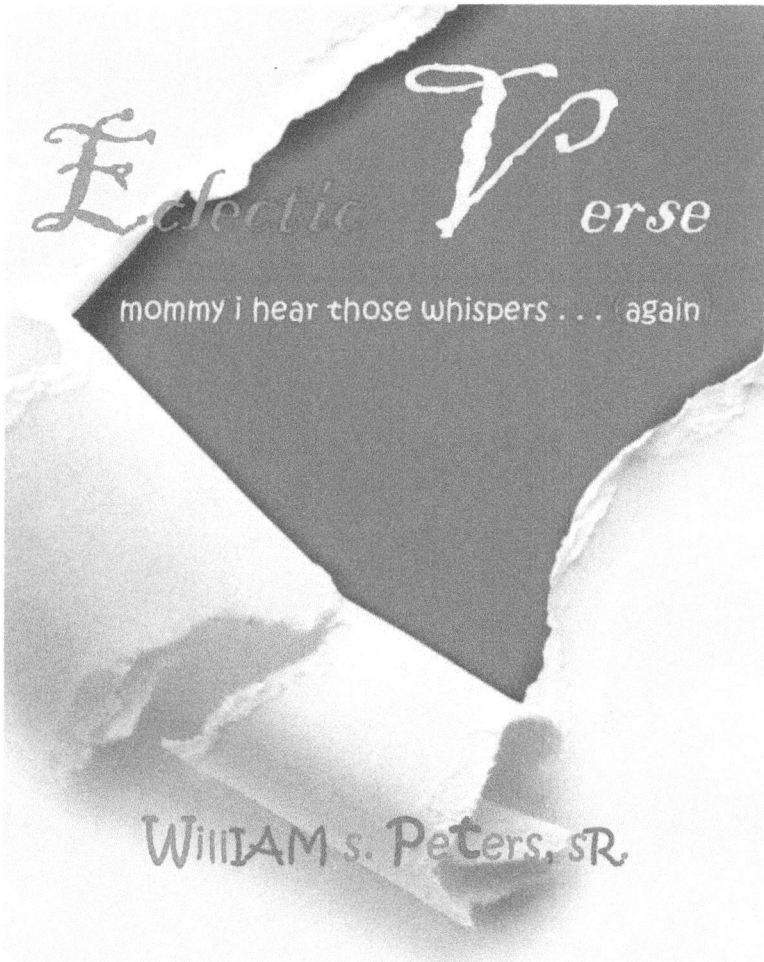

Eclectic Verse

mommy i hear those whispers . . . again

WiLLiAM s. PeTers, sR.

HERENOW

FAHREDIN SHEHU

Now Available at
www.innerchildpress.com

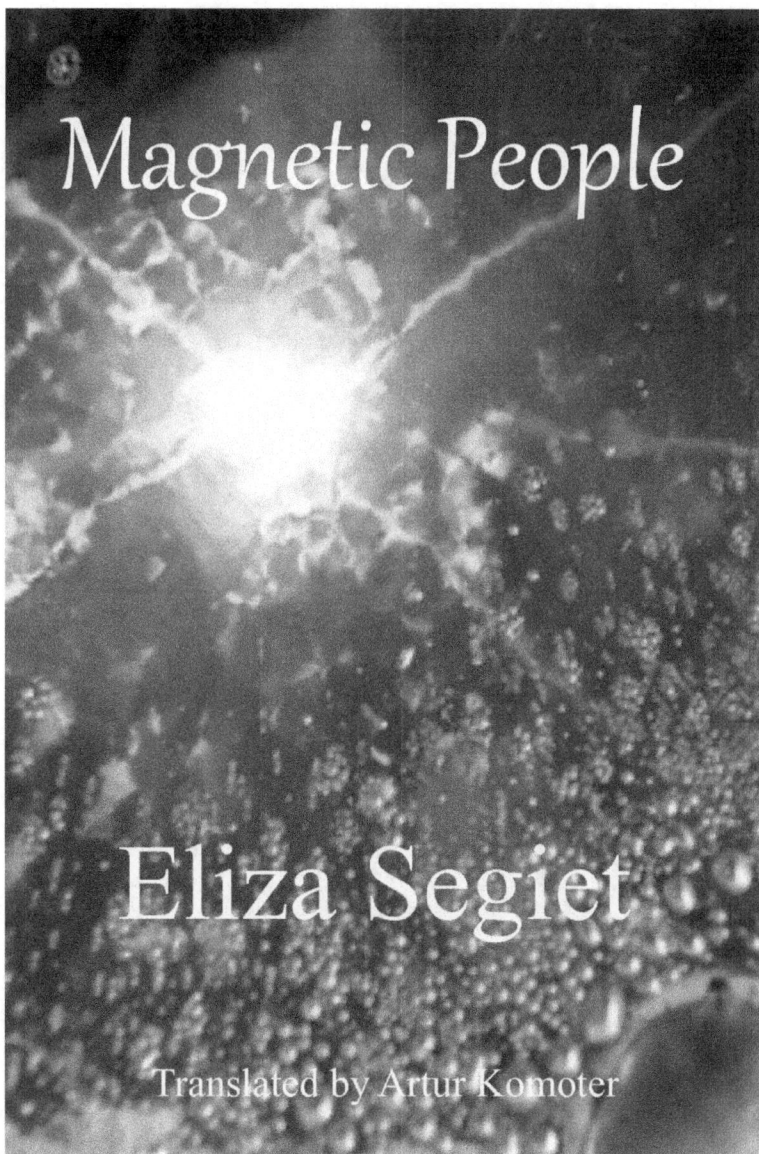

Magnetic People

Eliza Segiet

Translated by Artur Komoter

Now Available at

www.innerchildpress.com

Now Available at
www.innerchildpress.com

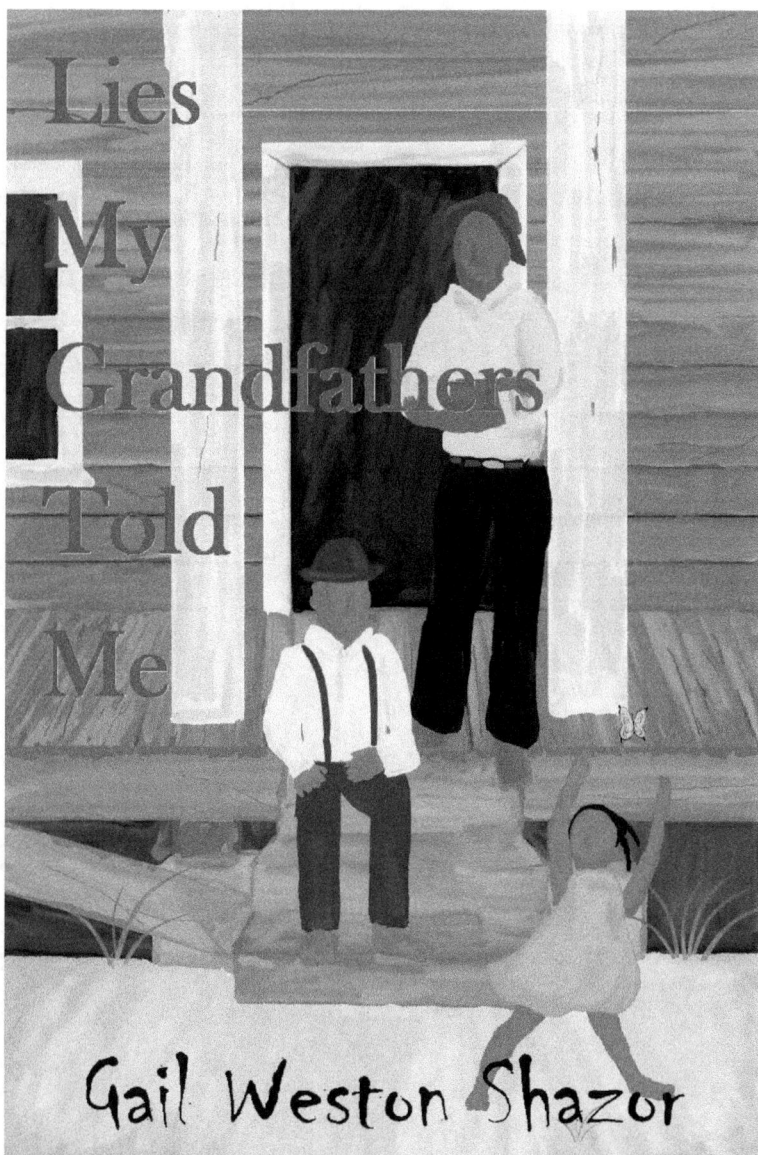

Lies
My
Grandfathers
Told
Me

Gail Weston Shazor

Now Available at
www.innerchildpress.com

Aflame

Memoirs in Verse

hülya n. yılmaz

My Shadow

Nizar Sartawi

Now Available at
www.innerchildpress.com

Mass Graves

Faleeha Hassan

Now Available at
www.innerchildpress.com

Breakfast

for

Butterflies

Faleeha Hassan

Now Available at
www.innerchildpress.com

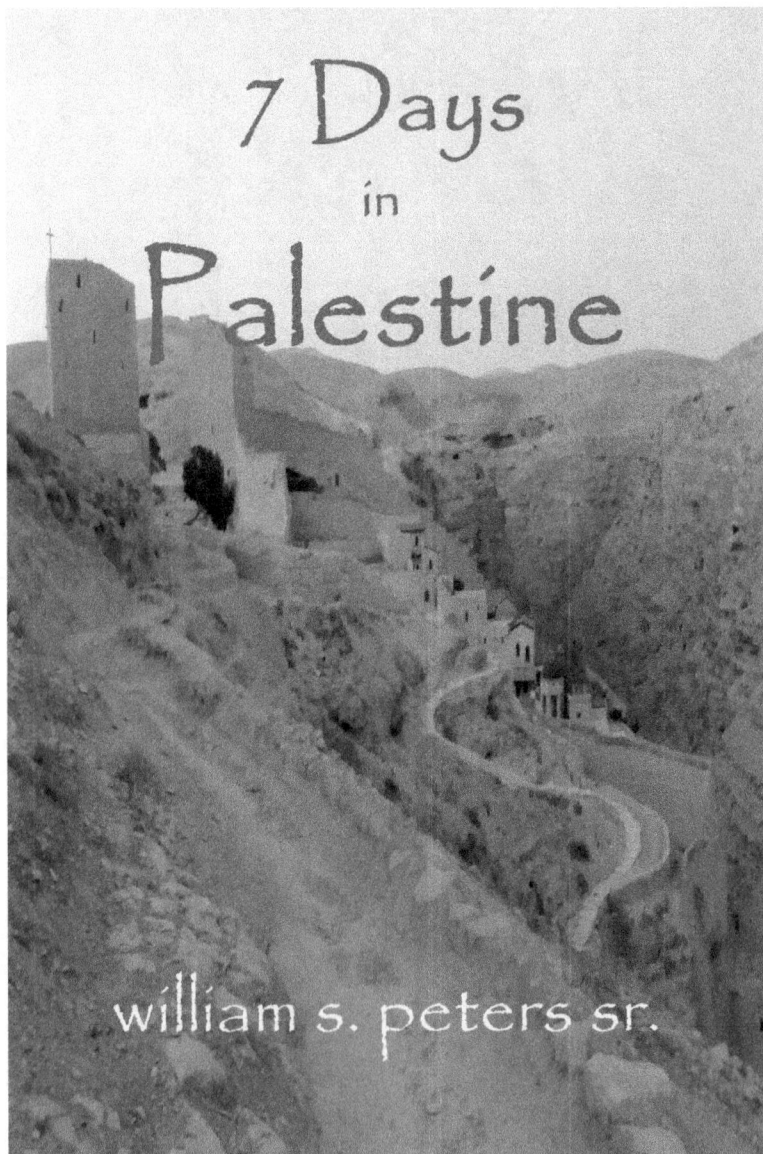

7 Days
in
Palestine

william s. peters sr.

Now Available at
www.innerchildpress.com

inner child press
presents

Tunisia My Love

william s. peters, sr.

Coming in the Summer of 2019

The Journey

Footprints and Shadows

Kosovo
Tunisia
Macedonia
Morocco
Jordan
Palestine
Israel
Italy
Turkey

a collection of poetry inspired during my travels

william s. peters, sr.

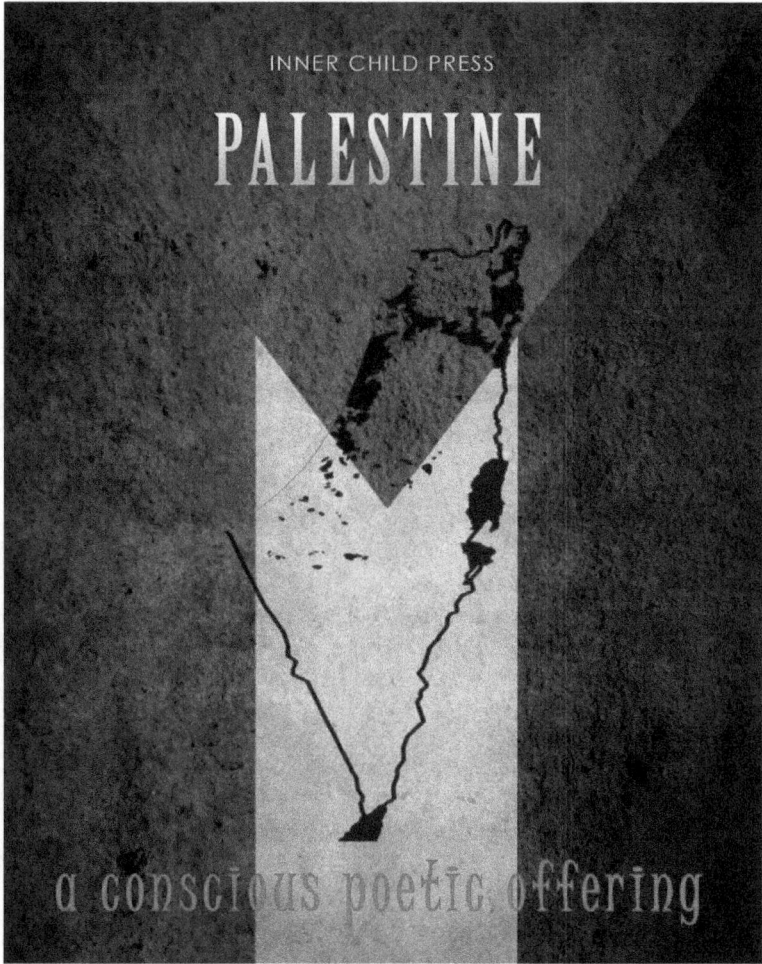

Now Available at

www.innerchildpress.com

Now Available at
www.innerchildpress.com

INNER CHILD PRESS

THIS IS WHY I
SLEEP

william s. peters sr.

Now Available at
www.innerchildpress.com

Think on These Things
Book II

william s. peters, sr.

Now Available at
www.innerchildpress.com

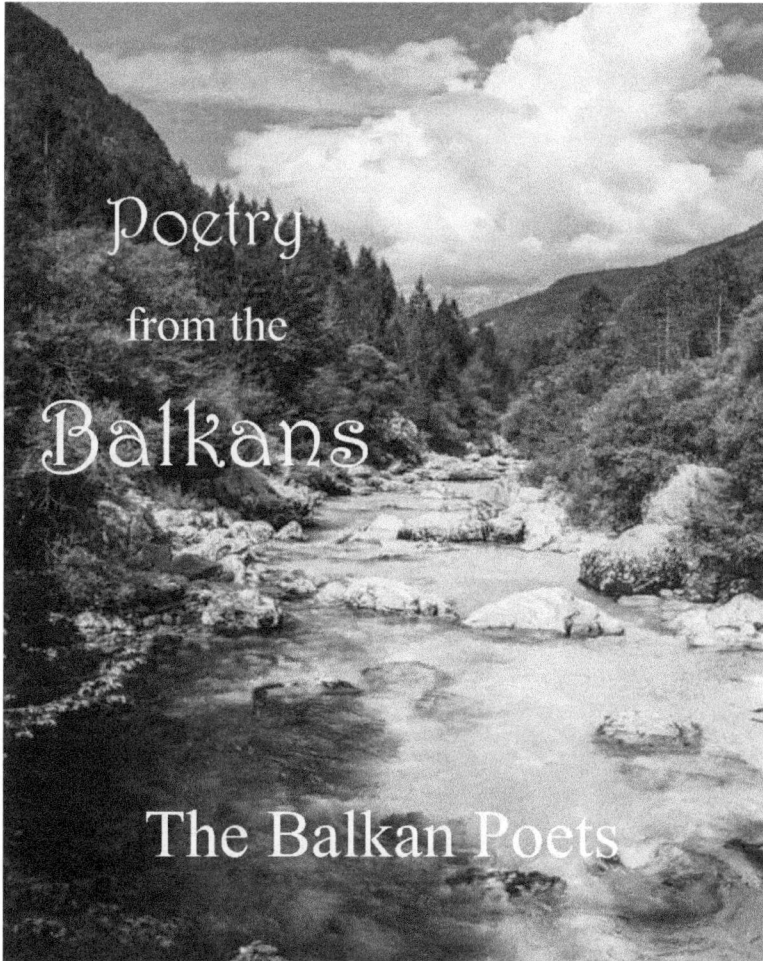

Poetry
from the
Balkans

The Balkan Poets

Other

Anthological

works from

Inner Child Press International

www.innerchildpress.com

Inner Child Press International
presents

A Love Anthology
2019

The Love Poets

Now Available

www.worldhealingworldpeacepoetry.com

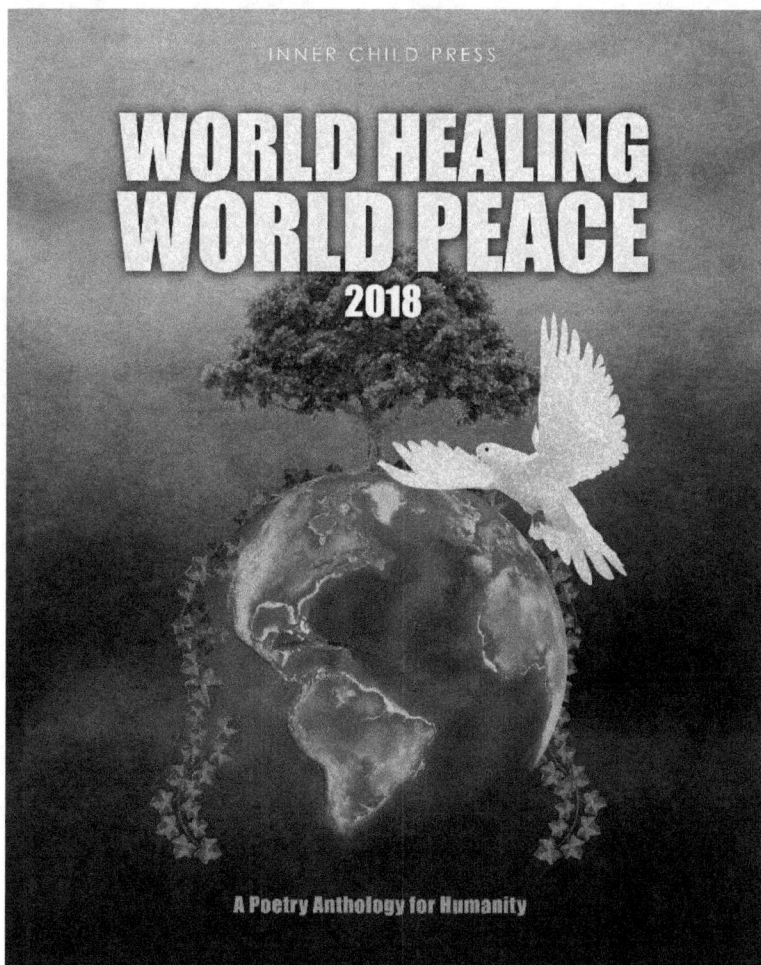

INNER CHILD PRESS

WORLD HEALING
WORLD PEACE
2018

A Poetry Anthology for Humanity

Now Available

www.worldhealingworldpeacepoetry.com

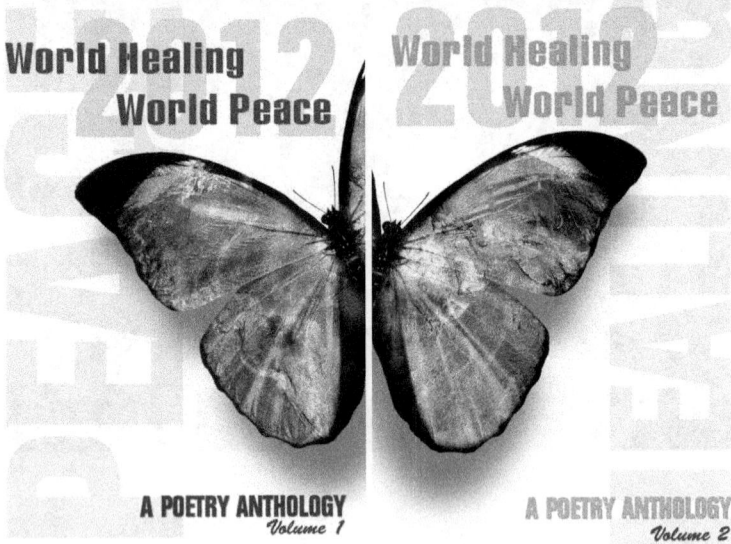

Now Available

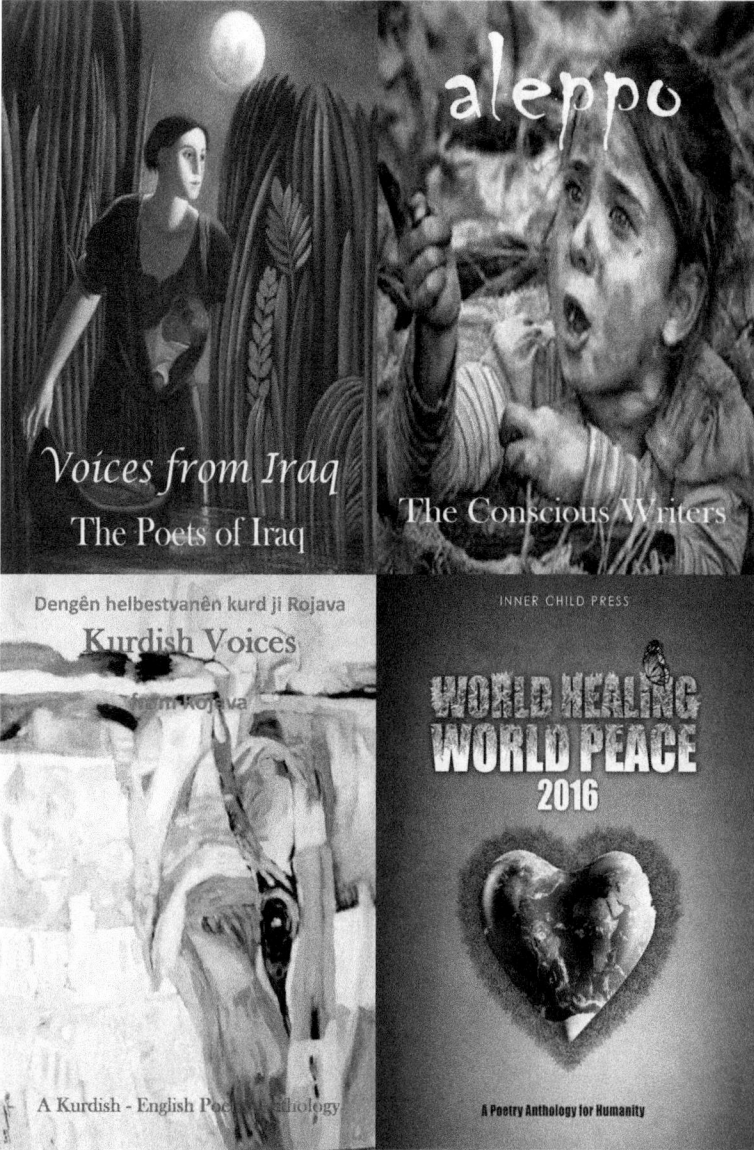

Voices from Iraq
The Poets of Iraq

aleppo
The Conscious Writers

Dengên helbestvanên kurd ji Rojava
Kurdish Voices
A Kurdish - English Poetry Anthology

INNER CHILD PRESS
WORLD HEALING
WORLD PEACE
2016
A Poetry Anthology for Humanity

Now Available

www.innerchildpress.com/anthologies

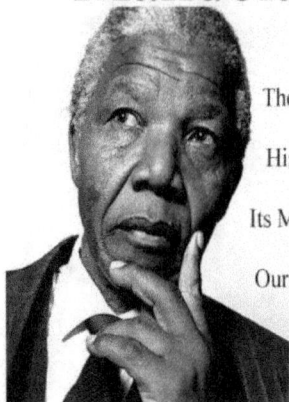

Mandela

The Man

His Life

Its Meaning

Our Words

Poetry . . . Commentary & Stories
The Anthological Writers

A GATHERING OF WORDS

POETRY & COMMENTARY
FOR
TRAYVON MARTIN

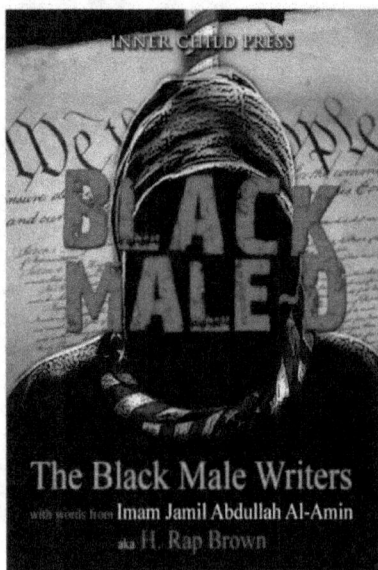

INNER CHILD PRESS

BLACK MALE-D

The Black Male Writers
with words from Imam Jamil Abdullah Al-Amin
aka H. Rap Brown

I want my poetry to... *volume* 4

the conscious poets
inspired by . . . Monte Smith

Now Available

www.innerchildpress.com/anthologies

Now Available

www.innerchildpress.com/anthologies

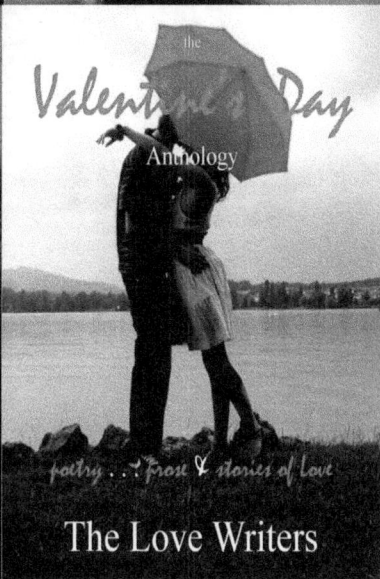

Janet
gone too soon . . .

healing through words

Poetry ...Prose ... Prayer ... Stories

a
Poetically
Spoken
Anthology
volume 1
Collector's Edition

The Poetry Posse
Presents

an anthology
of

Love

The Poetry Posse 2016

Now Available

www.innerchildpress.com/anthologies

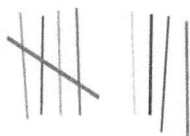

Now Available

www.innerchildpress.com/anthologies

The Year of the Poet
January 2014

The Poetry Posse

Jamie Bond
Gail Weston Shazor
Albert 'Infinite' Carrasco
Siddartha Beth Pierce
Janet P. Caldwell
June 'Bugg' Barefield
Debbie M. Allen
Tony Henninger
Joe DaVerbal Minddancer
Robert Gibbons
Neetu Wali
Shareef Abdur-Rasheed
William S. Peters, Sr.

Carnation

Our January Feature
Terri L. Johnson

the Year of the Poet
February 2014

violets

The Poetry Posse

Jamie Bond
Gail Weston Shazor
Albert 'Infinite' Carrasco
Siddartha Beth Pierce
Janet P. Caldwell
June 'Bugg' Barefield
Debbie M. Allen
Tony Henninger
Joe DaVerbal Minddancer
Robert Gibbons
Neetu Wali
Shareef Abdur-Rasheed
William S. Peters, Sr.

Our February Features
Teresa E. Gallion & Robert Gibson

the Year of the Poet
March 2014

The Poetry Posse

Jamie Bond
Gail Weston Shazor
Albert 'Infinite' Carrasco
Siddartha Beth Pierce
Janet P. Caldwell
June 'Bugg' Barefield
Debbie M. Allen
Tony Henninger
Joe DaVerbal Minddancer
Robert Gibbons
Neetu Wali
Shareef Abdur-Rasheed
Kimberly Burnham
William S. Peters, Sr.

daffodil

Our March Featured Poets
Alicia C. Cooper & Julya yilmaz

the Year of the Poet
April 2014

The Poetry Posse

Jamie Bond
Gail Weston Shazor
Albert 'Infinite' Carrasco
Siddartha Beth Pierce
Janet P. Caldwell
June 'Bugg' Barefield
Debbie M. Allen
Tony Henninger
Joe DaVerbal Minddancer
Robert Gibbons
Neetu Wali
Shareef Abdur-Rasheed
Kimberly Burnham
William S. Peters, Sr.

Our April Featured Poets
Fahredin Shehu
Martina Reisz Newberry
Justin Blackburn
Monte Smith

Sweet Pea

celebrating international poetry month

Now Available

www.innerchildpress.com/the-year-of-the-poet

176

the year of the poet
May 2014

May's Featured Poets

ReeCee
Joski the Poet
Shannon Stanton

Dedicated To our Children

The Poetry Posse

Jamie Bond
Gail Weston Shazor
Albert 'Infinite' Carrasco
Siddartha Beth Pierce
Janet P. Caldwell
Jamie 'Bugg' Barefield
Debbie M. Allen
Tony Henninger
Joe DeVerbal Minddancer
Robert Gibbons
Neetu Wali
Shareef Abdur-Rasheed
Kimberly Burnham
William S. Peters, Sr.

Lily of the Valley

the Year of the Poet
June 2014

Love & Relationship

Rose

June's Featured Poets

Shantelle McLin
Jacqueline D. E. Kennedy
Abraham N. Benjamin

The Poetry Posse

Jamie Bond
Gail Weston Shazor
Albert Infinite' Carrasco
Siddartha Beth Pierce
Janet P. Caldwell
June 'Bugg' Barefield
Debbie M. Allen
Tony Henninger
Joe DeVerbal Minddancer
Robert Gibbons
Neetu Wali
Shareef Abdur-Rasheed
Kimberly Burnham
William S. Peters, Sr.

The Year of the Poet
July 2014

July Feature Poets

Christena A.V. Williams
Dr. John R. Strum
Kolade Olanrewaju Freedom

The Poetry Posse

Jamie Bond
Gail Weston Shazor
Albert 'Infinite' Carrasco
Siddartha Beth Pierce
Janet P. Caldwell
June 'Bugg' Barefield
Debbie M. Allen
Tony Henninger
Joe DeVerbal Minddancer
Robert Gibbons
Neetu Wali
Shareef Abdur-Rasheed
Kimberly Burnham
William S. Peters, Sr.

Lotus
Asian Flower of the Month

The Year of the Poet
August 2014

Gladiolus

The Poetry Posse

Jamie Bond
Gail Weston Shazor
Albert 'Infinite' Carrasco
Siddartha Beth Pierce
Janet P. Caldwell
June 'Bugg' Barefield
Debbie M. Allen
Tony Henninger
Joe DeVerbal Minddancer
Robert Gibbons
Neetu Wali
Shareef Abdur-Rasheed
Kimberly Burnham
William S. Peters, Sr.

August Feature Poets

Ann White * Rosalind Cherry * Sheila Jenkins

Now Available

www.innerchildpress.com/the-year-of-the-poet

The Year of the Poet
September 2014

Aster · Morning-Glory

Wild Chaparral September Birthday Flower

September Feature Poets
Florence Malone · Keith Alan Hamilton

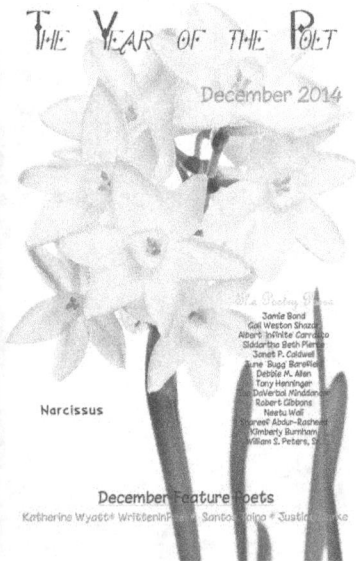

The Poetry Posse
Jamie Bond · Gail Weston Shazor · Albert 'Infinite' Carrasco · Siddartha Beth Pierce
Janet P. Caldwell · June 'Bugg' Barefield · Debbie M. Allen · Tony Henninger
Joe DaVerbal Minddancer · Robert Gibbons · Neetu Wali · Shareef Abdur-Rasheed
Kimberly Burnham · William S. Peters, Sr.

THE YEAR OF THE POET
October 2014

Red Poppy

The Poetry Posse
Jamie Bond · Gail Weston Shazor · Albert 'Infinite' Carrasco · Siddartha Beth Pierce
Janet P. Caldwell · June 'Bugg' Barefield · Debbie M. Allen · Tony Henninger
Joe DaVerbal Minddancer · Robert Gibbons · Neetu Wali · Shareef Abdur-Rasheed
Kimberly Burnham · William S. Peters, Sr.

October Feature Poets
Ceri Naz · Rajendra Padhi · Elizabeth Castillo

THE YEAR OF THE POET
November 2014

Chrysanthemum

The Poetry Posse
Jamie Bond · Gail Weston Shazor · Albert 'Infinite' Carrasco · Siddartha Beth Pierce
Janet P. Caldwell · June 'Bugg' Barefield · Debbie M. Allen · Tony Henninger
Joe DaVerbal Minddancer · Robert Gibbons · Neetu Wali · Shareef Abdur-Rasheed
Kimberly Burnham · William S. Peters, Sr.

November Feature Poets
Jocelyn Mosman · Jackie Allen · James Moore · Neville Hiatt

THE YEAR OF THE POET
December 2014

Narcissus

The Poetry Posse
Jamie Bond
Gail Weston Shazor
Albert Infinite Carrasco
Siddartha Beth Pierce
Janet P. Caldwell
June 'Bugg' Barefield
Debbie M. Allen
Tony Henninger
DaVerbal Minddancer
Robert Gibbons
Neetu Wali
Shareef Abdur-Rasheed
Kimberly Burnham
William S. Peters, S.

December Feature Poets
Katherine Wyatt· WritteninPeace · Santos Molina · Justin Clarke

Now Available

www.innerchildpress.com/the-year-of-the-poet

The Year of the Poet II

January 2015

Garnet

The Poetry Posse

Jamie Bond
Gail Weston Shazor
Albert 'Infinite' Carrasco
Siddartha Beth Pierce
Janet P. Caldwell
Tony Henninger
Joe DaVerbal Minddancer
Robert Gibbons
Neetu Wali
Shareef Abdur – Rasheed
Kimberly Burnham
Ann White
Keith Alan Hamilton
Katherine Wyatt
Fahredin Shehu
Hülya N. Yılmaz
Teresa E. Gallion
Jackie Allen
William S. Peters, Sr.

January Feature Poets
Bismay Mohanti * Jen Walls * Eric Judah

THE YEAR OF THE POET II

February 2015

Amethyst

THE POETRY POSSE

Jamie Bond
Gail Weston Shazor
Albert 'Infinite' Carrasco
Siddartha Beth Pierce
Janet P. Caldwell
Tony Henninger
Joe DaVerbal Minddancer
Robert Gibbons
Neetu Wali
Shareef Abdur – Rasheed
Kimberly Burnham
Ann White
Keith Alan Hamilton
Katherine Wyatt
Fahredin Shehu
Hülya N. Yılmaz
Teresa E. Gallion
Jackie Allen
William S. Peters, Sr.

FEBRUARY FEATURE POETS
Iram Fatima * Bob McNeil * Kerstin Centervall

The Year of the Poet II

March 2015

Our Featured Poets

Heung Sook * Anthony Arnold * Alicia Poland

Bloodstone

The Poetry Posse 2015
Jamie Bond * Gail Weston Shazor * Albert 'Infinite' Carrasco
Siddartha Beth Pierce * Janet P. Caldwell * Tony Henninger
Joe DaVerbal Minddancer * Neetu Wali * Shareef Abdur – Rasheed
Kimberly Burnham * Ann White * Keith Alan Hamilton
Katherine Wyatt * Fahredin Shehu * Hülya N. Yılmaz
Teresa E. Gallion * Jackie Allen * William S. Peters, Sr.

The Year of the Poet II

April 2015

Celebrating International Poetry Month

Our Featured Poets

Raja Williams * Dennis Ferado * Laure Charazac

Diamonds

The Poetry Posse 2015
Jamie Bond * Gail Weston Shazor * Albert 'Infinite' Carrasco
Siddartha Beth Pierce * Janet P. Caldwell * Tony Henninger
Joe DaVerbal Minddancer * Neetu Wali * Shareef Abdur – Rasheed
Kimberly Burnham * Ann White * Keith Alan Hamilton
Katherine Wyatt * Fahredin Shehu * Hülya N. Yılmaz
Teresa E. Gallion * Jackie Allen * William S. Peters, Sr.

Now Available

www.innerchildpress.com/the-year-of-the-poet

The Year of the Poet II
May 2015

May's Featured Poets
Geri Algeri
Akin Mosi Chinnery
Anna Jakubeza

Emeralds

The Poetry Posse 2015
Jamie Bond * Gail Weston Shazor * Albert 'Infinite' Carrasco
Siddartha Beth Pierce * Janet P. Caldwell * Tony Henninger
Joe DaVerbal Minddancer * Neetu Wali * Shareef Abdur – Rasheed
Kimberly Burnham * Ann White * Keith Alan Hamilton
Katherine Wyatt * Fahredin Shehu * Hülya N. Yılmaz
Teresa E. Gallion * Jackie Allen * William S. Peters, Sr.

The Year of the Poet II
June 2015

June's Featured Poets
Anahit Arustamyan * Yvette D. Murrell * Regina A. Walker

Pearl

The Poetry Posse 2015
Jamie Bond * Gail Weston Shazor * Albert 'Infinite' Carrasco
Siddartha Beth Pierce * Janet P. Caldwell * Tony Henninger
Joe DaVerbal Minddancer * Neetu Wali * Shareef Abdur – Rasheed
Kimberly Burnham * Ann White * Keith Alan Hamilton
Katherine Wyatt * Fahredin Shehu * Hülya N. Yılmaz
Teresa E. Gallion * Jackie Allen * William S. Peters, Sr.

The Year of the Poet II
July 2015

The Featured Poets for July 2015
Abhik Shome * Christina Neal * Robert Neal

Rubies

The Poetry Posse 2015
Jamie Bond * Gail Weston Shazor * Albert 'Infinite' Carrasco
Siddartha Beth Pierce * Janet P. Caldwell * Tony Henninger
Joe DaVerbal Minddancer * Neetu Wali * Shareef Abdur – Rasheed
Kimberly Burnham * Ann White * Keith Alan Hamilton
Katherine Wyatt * Fahredin Shehu * Hülya N. Yılmaz
Teresa E. Gallion * Jackie Allen * William S. Peters, Sr.

The Year of the Poet II
August 2015

Peridot

Featured Poets
Gayle Howell
Ann Chalasz
Christopher Schultz

The Poetry Posse 2015
Jamie Bond * Gail Weston Shazor * Albert 'Infinite' Carrasco
Siddartha Beth Pierce * Janet P. Caldwell * Tony Henninger
Joe DaVerbal Minddancer * Neetu Wali * Shareef Abdur – Rasheed
Kimberly Burnham * Ann White * Keith Alan Hamilton
Katherine Wyatt * Fahredin Shehu * Hülya N. Yılmaz
Teresa E. Gallion * Jackie Allen * William S. Peters, Sr.

Now Available

www.innerchildpress.com/the-year-of-the-poet

The Year of the Poet II
September 2015

Featured Poets

Alfreda Ghee · Lonneice Weeks Badley · Demetrios Trifiatis

Sapphires

The Poetry Posse 2015

Jamie Bond * Gail Weston Shazor * Albert 'Infinite' Carrasco
Siddartha Beth Pierce * Janet P. Caldwell * Tony Henninger
Joe DaVerbal Minddancer * Neetu Wali * Shareef Abdur – Rasheed
Kimberly Burnham * Ann White * Keith Alan Hamilton
Katherine Wyatt * Fahredin Shehu * Hülya N. Yilmaz
Teresa E. Gallion * Jackie Allen * William S. Peters, Sr.

The Year of the Poet II
October 2015

Featured Poets

Monte Smith * Laura J. Wolfe * William Washington

Opal

The Poetry Posse 2015

Jamie Bond * Gail Weston Shazor * Albert 'Infinite' Carrasco
Siddartha Beth Pierce * Janet P. Caldwell * Tony Henninger
Joe DaVerbal Minddancer * Neetu Wali * Shareef Abdur – Rasheed
Kimberly Burnham * Ann White * Keith Alan Hamilton
Katherine Wyatt * Fahredin Shehu * Hülya N. Yilmaz
Teresa E. Gallion * Jackie Allen * William S. Peters, Sr.

The Year of the Poet II
November 2015

Featured Poets

Alan W. Jankowski
Bismay Mohanty
James Moore

Topaz

The Poetry Posse 2015

Jamie Bond * Gail Weston Shazor * Albert 'Infinite' Carrasco
Siddartha Beth Pierce * Janet P. Caldwell * Tony Henninger
Joe DaVerbal Minddancer * Neetu Wali * Shareef Abdur – Rasheed
Kimberly Burnham * Ann White * Keith Alan Hamilton
Katherine Wyatt * Fahredin Shehu * Hülya N. Yilmaz
Teresa E. Gallion * Jackie Allen * William S. Peters, Sr.

The Year of the Poet II
December 2015

Featured Poets

Kerione Bryan * Michelle Joan Barulich * Neville Hiatt

Turquoise

The Poetry Posse 2015

Jamie Bond * Gail Weston Shazor * Albert 'Infinite' Carrasco
Siddartha Beth Pierce * Janet P. Caldwell * Tony Henninger
Joe DaVerbal Minddancer * Neetu Wali * Shareef Abdur – Rasheed
Kimberly Burnham * Ann White * Keith Alan Hamilton
Katherine Wyatt * Fahredin Shehu * Hülya N. Yilmaz
Teresa E. Gallion * Jackie Allen * William S. Peters, Sr.

Now Available

www.innerchildpress.com/the-year-of-the-poet

The Year of the Poet III
January 2016

Featured Poets
Lana Joseph * Atom Cyrus Rush * Christena Williams

Dark-eyed Junco

The Poetry Posse 2016
Gail Weston Shazor * Jhon Jakubezak Vel Ratysfdelm * Hno J. White
Fahredin Shehu * Hrishikesh Padhye * Janet P. Caldwell
Joe DaVerbal Minddancer * Shareef Abdur - Rasheed
Albert Carrasco * Kimberly Burnham * Keith Alan Hamilton
Hulya N. Yilmaz * Demetrios Trifiatis * Alan W. Jankowski
Teresa E. Gallion * Jackie Davis Allen * William S. Peters, Sr

The Year of the Poet III
February 2016

Featured Poets
Anthony Arnold
Anna Chalasz
DeAndre Hawthorne

Puffin

The Poetry Posse 2016
Gail Weston Shazor * Joe DaVerbal Minddancer * Alfreda Ghee
Fahredin Shehu * Hrishikesh Padhye * Janet P. Caldwell
Anna Jakubczak Vel Ratty Adalan * Shareef Abdur - Rasheed
Albert Carrasco * Kimberly Burnham * Hno J. White
Hulya N. Yilmaz * Demetrios Trifiatis * Alan W. Jankowski
Teresa E. Gallion * Jackie Davis Allen * William S. Peters, Sr

The Year of the Poet
March 2016
Featured Poets
Jeton Kelmendi   Nizar Sartawi   Sami Muhanna

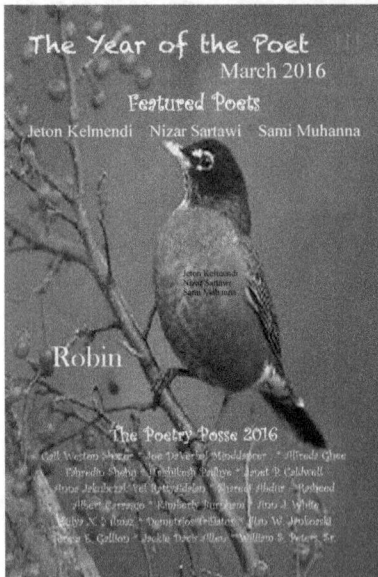

Robin

The Poetry Posse 2016
Gail Weston Shazor * Joe DaVerbal Minddancer * Alfreda Ghee
Fahredin Shehu * Hrishikesh Padhye * Janet P. Caldwell
Anna Jakubczak Vel Ratty Adalan * Shareef Abdur - Rasheed
Albert Carrasco * Kimberly Burnham * Hno J. White
Hulya N. Yilmaz * Demetrios Trifiatis * Alan W. Jankowski
Teresa E. Gallion * Jackie Davis Allen * William S. Peters, Sr

The Year of the Poet III

Featured Poets
Ali Abdolrezaei
Anna Chalasz
Agim Vinca
Ceri Naz

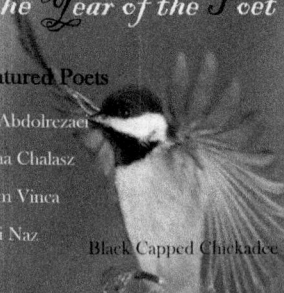

Black Capped Chickadee

The Poetry Posse 2016
Gail Weston Shazor * Joe DaVerbal Minddancer * Alfreda Ghee
Fahredin Shehu * Hrishikesh Padhye * Janet P. Caldwell
Anna Jakubczak Vel Ratty Adalan * Shareef Abdur - Rasheed
Albert Carrasco * Kimberly Burnham * Ann J. White
Hulya N. Yilmaz * Demetrios Trifiatis * Alan W. Jankowski
Teresa E. Gallion * Jackie Davis Allen * William S. Peters, Sr

celebrating international poetry month

Now Available

www.innerchildpress.com/the-year-of-the-poet

The Year of the Poet
May 2016

Bob Strum
Barbara Allan
D.L. Davis

Oriole

The Poetry Posse 2016

The Year of the Poet III
June 2016

Featured Poets

Qibrije Demiri- Frangu
Naime Beqiraj
Faleeba Hassan
Bedri Zyberaj

Black Necked Sult

The Poetry Posse 2016

The Year of the Poet III
July 2016

Iram Fatima 'Ashi'
Langley Shazor
Jody Doty
Emilia T. Davis

Indigo Bunting

The Poetry Posse 2016

The Year of the Poet III
August 2016

Featured Poets

Anita Dash
Irena Jovanovic
Malgorzata Gouluda

Painted Bunting

The Poetry Posse 2016

Now Available

www.innerchildpress.com/the-year-of-the-poet

The Year of the Poet III
September 2016

Featured Poets

Simone Weber
Abhijit Sen
Eunice Barbara C Novio

Long Billed Curle

The Poetry Posse 2016

The Year of the Poet III
October 2016

Featured Poets

Jann Joseph
Krishnamurthy
James Moore

Barn Owl

The Poetry Posse 2016

The Year of the Poet III
November 2016

Featured Poets

Rosemary Burns
Robin Ouzman Hislop
Lonneice Weeks-Badler

Northern Cardinal

The Poetry Posse 2016

The Year of the Poet III
December 2016

Featured Poets

Samíh Masoud
Mountassir Aziz Bien
Abdulkadir Musa

Rough Legged Hawk

The Poetry Posse 2016

Now Available

www.innerchildpress.com/the-year-of-the-poet

The Year of the Poet IV
May 2017

The Flowering Dogwood Tree

Featured Poets
Kallisa Powell
Alicja Maria Kuberska
Fethi Sassi

The Poetry Posse 2017

Gail Weston Shazor * Caroline Nazareno * Bismay Mohanty
Teresa E. Gallion * Anna Jakubczak Vel Ratty Adalan
Joe DaVerbal Minddancer * Shareef Abdur - Rasheed
Albert Carrasco * Kimberly Burnham * Elizabeth Castillo
Hülya N. Yılmaz * Fahredin Shehu * Jackie Davis Allen
Jen Walls * Nizar Sartawi * * William S. Peters, Sr.

The Year of the Poet IV
June 2017

Featured Poets
Eliza Segiet
Tze-Min Tsai
Abdulla Issa

The Linden Tree

The Poetry Posse 2017

Hülya N. Yılmaz *
Jen Walls * Nizar Sartawi * William S. Peters, Sr.

The Year of the Poet IV
July 2017

Featured Poets
Anca Mihaela Bruma
Ibaa Ismail
Zvonko Taneski

The Oak Moon

The Poetry Posse 2017

Gail Weston Shazor *
Teresa E. Gallion * Anna Jakubczak Vel Ratty Adalan
Joe DaVerbal Minddancer * Shareef Abdur - Rasheed
Albert Carrasco * Kimberly Burnham * Elizabeth Castillo
Hülya N. Yılmaz * Fahredin Shehu * Jackie Davis Allen
Jen Walls * Nizar Sartawi * * William S. Peters, Sr.

The Year of the Poet IV
August 2017

Featured Poets
Jonathan Aquino
Kitty Hsu
Langley Shazor

The Hazelnut Tree

The Poetry Posse 2017

Gail Weston Shazor * Caroline Nazareno *
Teresa E. Gallion * Anna Jakubczak Vel Ratty Adalan
Joe DaVerbal Minddancer * Shareef Abdur - Rasheed
Albert Carrasco * Kimberly Burnham * Elizabeth Castillo
Hülya N. Yılmaz * Fahredin Shehu * Jackie Davis Allen
Jen Walls * Nizar Sartawi * * William S. Peters, Sr.

Now Available

www.innerchildpress.com/the-year-of-the-poet

The Year of the Poet IV
September 2017

Featured Poets

Martina Reisz Newberry
Ameer Nassir
Christine Fulco Neal
Robert Neal

The Elm Tree

The Poetry Posse 2017

Gail Weston Shazor * Caroline Nazareno * Bismay Mohanty
Teresa E. Gallion * Anna Jakubczak Vel Ratty Adalan
Joe DaVerbal Minddancer * Shareef Abdur – Rasheed
Albert Carrasco * Kimberly Burnham * Elizabeth Castillo
Hülya N. Yılmaz * Faleeha Hassan * Jackie Davis Allen
Jen Walls * Nizar Sartawi * * William S. Peters, Sr.

The Year of the Poet IV
October 2017

Featured Poets

Ahmed Abu Saleem
Nedal Al-Qaeim
Sadeddin Shahin

The Black Walnut Tree

The Poetry Posse 2017

Gail Weston Shazor * Caroline Nazareno * Bismay Mohanty
Teresa E. Gallion * Anna Jakubczak Vel Ratty Adalan
Joe DaVerbal Minddancer * Shareef Abdur – Rasheed
Albert Carrasco * Kimberly Burnham * Elizabeth Castillo
Hülya N. Yılmaz * Faleeha Hassan * Jackie Davis Allen
Jen Walls * Nizar Sartawi * * William S. Peters, Sr.

The Year of the Poet IV
November 2017

Featured Poets

Kay Peters
Alfreda D. Ghee
Gabriella Garofalo
Rosemary Cappello

The Tree of Life

The Poetry Posse 2017

Gail Weston Shazor * Caroline Nazareno * Bismay Mohanty
Teresa E. Gallion * Anna Jakubczak Vel Ratty Adalan
Joe DaVerbal Minddancer * Shareef Abdur – Rasheed
Albert Carrasco * Kimberly Burnham * Elizabeth Castillo
Hülya N. Yılmaz * Faleeha Hassan * Jackie Davis Allen
Jen Walls * Nizar Sartawi * William S. Peters, Sr.

The Year of the Poet IV
December 2017

Featured Poets

Justice Clarke
Mariel M. Pabroa
Kiley Brown

The Fig Tree

The Poetry Posse 2017

Gail Weston Shazor * Caroline Nazareno * Bismay Mohanty
Teresa E. Gallion * Anna Jakubczak Vel Ratty Adalan
Joe DaVerbal Minddancer * Shareef Abdur – Rasheed
Albert Carrasco * Kimberly Burnham * Elizabeth Castillo
Hülya N. Yılmaz * Faleeha Hassan * Jackie Davis Allen
Jen Walls * Nizar Sartawi * William S. Peters, Sr.

Now Available

www.innerchildpress.com/the-year-of-the-poet

The Year of the Poet V
January 2018
Featured Poets
Iyad Shamasnuh
Yasmeen Hamzeh
Ali Abdolrezaei

Aksum

The Poetry Posse 2018
Gail Weston Shazor * Caroline Nazareno * Tezmin Ition Tsai
Hülya N. Yılmaz * Faleeha Hassan * Jackie Davis Allen
Teresa E. Gallion * Anna Jakubczak Vel Ratty Adalan
Alicja Maria Kubenska * Shareef Abdur – Rasheed
Kimberly Burnham * Elizabeth Castillo
Nizar Sartawi * William S. Peters, Sr.

The Year of the Poet V
February 2018

Sabean

Featured Poets
Muhammad Azram
Anna Szawracka
Abhilipsa Kuanar
Aanika Aery

The Poetry Posse 2018
Gail Weston Shazor * Caroline Nazareno * Tezmin Ition Tsai
Hülya N. Yılmaz * Faleeha Hassan * Jackie Davis Allen
Teresa E. Gallion * Anna Jakubczak Vel Ratty Adalan
Alicja Maria Kubenska * Shareef Abdur – Rasheed
Kimberly Burnham * Elizabeth Castillo
Nizar Sartawi * William S. Peters, Sr.

The Year of the Poet V
March 2018

Featured Poets
Iram Fatima 'Ashi'
Cassandra Swan
Jaleel Khazaal
Shazin Zaman

The Poetry Posse 2018
Gail Weston Shazor * Nizar Sartawi * Hülya N. Yılmaz
Jackie Davis Allen * Caroline 'Ceri' Nazareno
Alicja Maria Kubenska * Teresa E. Gallion
Faleeha Hassan * Shareef Abdur – Rasheed
Kimberly Burnham * Elizabeth Castillo
Tezmin Ition Tsai * William S. Peters, Sr.

The Year of the Poet V
April 2018

The Nez Perce

Now Available

www.innerchildpress.com/the-year-of-the-poet

Now Available

www.innerchildpress.com/the-year-of-the-poet

The Year of the Poet V
September 2018

The Aztecs & Incas

Featured Poets
Kolade Olanrewaju Freedom
Eliza Segiet
Mazher Hussain Abdul Ghani
Lily Swarn

The Poetry Posse 2018
Gail Weston Shazor * Nizar Sartawi * Hülya N. Yılmaz
Jackie Davis Allen * Caroline 'Ceri' Nazareno
Alicja Maria Kuberska * Teresa E. Gallion
Kimberly Burnham * Shareef Abdur – Rasheed
Ashok K. Bhargava * Elizabeth Castillo * Swapna Behera
Tezmin Ition Tsai * William S. Peters, Sr.

The Year of the Poet V
October 2018

Featured Poets
Alicia Minjarez * Lonneice Weeks-Badley
Lopamudra Mishra * Abdelwahed Souayah

Bengali

The Poetry Posse 2018
Gail Weston Shazor * Nizar Sartawi * Hülya N. Yılmaz
Jackie Davis Allen * Caroline 'Ceri' Nazareno
Alicja Maria Kuberska * Teresa E. Gallion
Kimberly Burnham * Shareef Abdur – Rasheed
Ashok K. Bhargava * Elizabeth Castillo * Swapna Behera
Tezmin Ition Tsai * William S. Peters, Sr.

The Year of the Poet V
November 2018

Featured Poets
Michelle Joan Barulich * Monsif Beroual
Krystyna Konecka * Nassira Nezzar

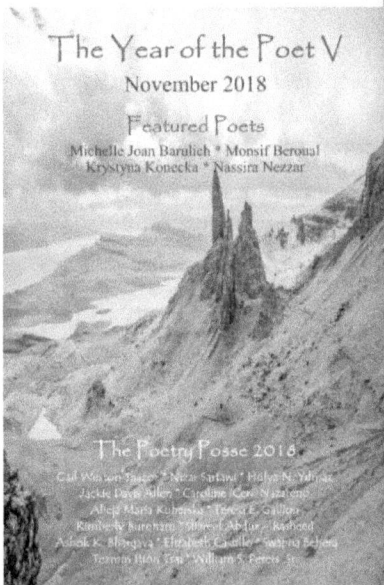

The Poetry Posse 2018
Gail Weston Shazor * Nizar Sartawi * Hülya N. Yılmaz
Jackie Davis Allen * Caroline 'Ceri' Nazareno
Alicja Maria Kuberska * Teresa E. Gallion
Kimberly Burnham * Shareef Abdur – Rasheed
Ashok K. Bhargava * Elizabeth Castillo * Swapna Behera
Tezmin Ition Tsai * William S. Peters, Sr.

The Year of the Poet V
December 2018

Featured Poets
Rose Terranova Cirigliano
Joanna Kalinowska
Sokolović Emin
Dr. T. Ashok Chakravarthy

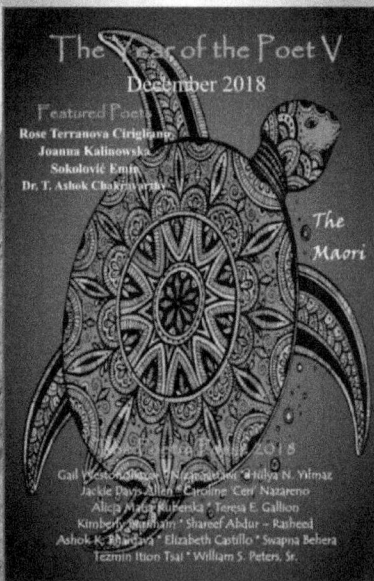

The Maori

The Poetry Posse 2018
Gail Weston Shazor * Nizar Sartawi * Hülya N. Yılmaz
Jackie Davis Allen * Caroline 'Ceri' Nazareno
Alicja Maria Kuberska * Teresa E. Gallion
Kimberly Burnham * Shareef Abdur – Rasheed
Ashok K. Bhargava * Elizabeth Castillo * Swapna Behera
Tezmin Ition Tsai * William S. Peters, Sr.

Now Available

www.innerchildpress.com/the-year-of-the-poet

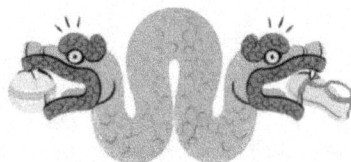

The Year of the Poet VI
May 2019

Featured Poets
Emad Al-Haydary * Hussein Nasser Jabr
Wahab Sheriff * Abdul Razzaq Al Ameeri

Asia Southeast Asia and Maritime Asia

The Poetry Posse 2019

Gail Weston Shazor * Albert Carrasco * Hülya N. Yılmaz
Jackie Davis Allen * Caroline Nazareno * Eliza Segiet
Alicja Maria Kuberska * Teresa E. Gallion * Joe Paire
Kimberly Burnham * Shareef Abdur – Rasheed
Ashok K. Bhargava * Elizabeth Castillo * Swapna Behera
Tezmin Ition Tsai * William S. Peters, Sr.

The Year of the Poet VI
June 2019

Featured Poets
Kate Gaudi Powiekszone * Sabaj Sabharwal
Iwu Jeff * Muhamed Abdel Aziz Shneis

Arctic
Circumpolar

The Poetry Posse 2019

Gail Weston Shazor * Albert Carrasco * Hülya N. Yılmaz
Jackie Davis Allen * Caroline Nazareno * Eliza Segiet
Alicja Maria Kuberska * Teresa E. Gallion * Joe Paire
Kimberly Burnham * Shareef Abdur – Rasheed
Ashok K. Bhargava * Elizabeth Castillo * Swapna Behera
Tezmin Ition Tsai * William S. Peters, Sr.

The Year of the Poet VI
Jul 2019

Featured Poets
Saadeddin Shahin * Andy Scott
Fahreldin Shehu * Alok Kuamr Ray

The Horn of Africa

Ethiopia   Djibouti

Somalia   Eritrea

The Poetry Posse 2019

Gail Weston Shazor * Albert Carrasco * Hülya N. Yılmaz
Jackie Davis Allen * Caroline Nazareno * Eliza Segiet
Alicja Maria Kuberska * Teresa E. Gallion * Joe Paire
Kimberly Burnham * Shareef Abdur – Rasheed
Ashok K. Bhargava * Elizabeth Castillo * Swapna Behera
Tezmin Ition Tsai * William S. Peters, Sr.

The Year of the Poet VI
August 2019

Featured Poets
Shola Balogun * Bharati Nayak
Monalisa Dash Dwibedy * Mbizo Chirasha

Coexist

Southwest Asia

The Poetry Posse 2019

Gail Weston Shazor * Albert Carrasco * Hülya N. Yılmaz
Jackie Davis Allen * Caroline Nazareno * Eliza Segiet
Alicja Maria Kuberska * Teresa E. Gallion * Joe Paire
Kimberly Burnham * Shareef Abdur – Rasheed
Ashok K. Bhargava * Elizabeth Castillo * Swapna Behera
Tezmin Ition Tsai * William S. Peters, Sr.

Now Available

www.innerchildpress.com/the-year-of-the-poet

and there is much, much more !

visit . . .

www.innerchildpress.com/antho
logies-sales-special.php

Also check out our Authors and
all the wonderful Books
Available at :

www.innerchildpress.com/autho
rs-pages

INNER CHILD PRESS

WORLD HEALING WORLD PEACE
2018

A Poetry Anthology for Humanity

Now Available

www.worldhealingworldpeacepoetry.com

Now Available

www.worldhealingworldpeacepoetry.com

World Healing
World Peace

i support

www.worldhealingworldpeacepoetry.com

196

World Healing
World Peace
2018

Now Available

www.worldhealingworldpeacepoetry.com

Inner Child Press International

'building bridges of cultural understanding'

Meet our Cultural Ambassadors

Fahredin Shehu Director of Cultural	**Faleha Hassan** Iraq – USA	**Elizabeth E. Castillo** Philippines	**Antoinette Coleman** Chicago Midwest USA	**Ananda Nepali** Nepal – Tibet Northern India
Kimberly Burnham Pacific Northwest USA	**Alicja Kuberska** Poland Eastern Europe	**Swapna Behera** India Southeast Asia	**Kolade O. Freedom** Nigeria West Africa	**Munsif Beraual** Morocco Northern Africa
Ashok K. Bhargava Canada	**Tzemin Ition Tsai** Republic of China Greater China	**Alicia M. Ramirez** Mexico Central America	**Christena AV Williams** Jamaica Caribbean	**Louise Hudon** Eastern Canada
Aziz Mountassir Morocco Northern Africa	**Shareef Abdur-Rasheed** Southeastern USA	**Laure Charazac** France Western Europe	**Mohammud Ikbal Harb** Lebanon Middle East	**Mohamed Abdel Aziz Shmeis** Egypt Middle East
Hilary Mainga Kenya Eastern Africa	**Josephus R. Johnson** Liberia			

www.innerchildpress.com

This Anthological Publication
is underwritten solely by

Inner Child Press

Inner Child Press is a Publishing Company Founded and Operated by Writers. Our personal publishing experiences provides us an intimate understanding of the sometimes daunting challenges Writers, New and Seasoned may face in the Business of Publishing and Marketing their Creative "Written Work".

For more Information

Inner Child Press

www.innerchildpress.com

Inner Child Press International

'building bridges of cultural understanding'
202 Wiltree Court, State College, Pennsylvania 16801

www.innerchildpress.com

200

~ fini ~

Coming
April 2020

The
World Healing, World Peace
International Poetry Symposium

Stay Tuned

for more information
intouch@innerchildpress.com
'building bridges of cultural understanding'
www.innerchildpress.com

www.ingramcontent.com/pod-product-compliance
Lightning Source LLC
LaVergne TN
LVHW051047080426
835508LV00019B/1756